D1217701

DATE			

BAKER & TAYLOR

TELECOMMUNICATIONS DEVELOPMENT

The Case of Africa

L. Kwabena Riverson, Ph.D.

UNIVERSITY
PRESS OF
AMERICA

Lanham • New York • London

Copyright © 1993 by
University Press of America® Inc.
4720 Boston Way
Lanham, Maryland 20706

3 Henrietta Street
London WC2E 8LU England

Library of Congress Cataloging-in-Publication Data
Riverson, L. Kwabena.
Telecommunications development : the case of Africa /
L. Kwabena Riverson.
p.   cm.
Includes bibliographical references and index.
1. Telecommunication—Africa.   2. Telecommunication policy—
Africa.   3. Pan-African Telecommunications Union.
4. Communication in rural development—Africa.   I. Title.
HE8464.R58   1993   384'.096—dc20   93–32751 CIP

ISBN 0–8191–9315–1 (cloth : alk. paper)

To my only daughter,
Afua Adobea Riverson

ACKNOWLEDGMENTS

I am a full believer of the notion "knowledge is power," and while seeking and contributing to this wisdom, I see myself falling in debt to many individuals and organizations with whom I associate. I wish to express my sincere thanks and appreciation to Dr. Robert Nwanko of Howard University in Washington, D.C., whose encouragement helped make this book successful.

Not to mention so many international organizations that provided support for this book. I am thus indebtted to the International Telecommunication Union (ITU), the Economic Commission for Africa (ECA), the International Telecommunications Satellite Organization (INTELSAT), The World Bank, and the Arab Satellite Organization (ARABSAT).

I would like to thank the reviewers and the publishing staff at the University Press of America, especially Helen Hudson and Julie Kirsch. As an author, I feel I was extremely fortunate to have them as my editors.

A word of thanks to my friends and colleagues who have contributed so much to my social and professional life, including: Constance Larbi, Suzanne Garland, Gloria Thomas, Dr. Ardelle Lllewellyn, and Dr. Kwaku Ofori Ansah.

It took longer than I expected, but there is no way that I could complete this book without the secretarial skills of Sheryl Bowlin, the proofreading expertise of Krista Rogers, and, of course, Barbara Stras who typeset the final manuscript for publication. Finally, I owe Ms. Lucille Brinson for all her motherly support.

L. Kwabena Riverson, Ph.D.

TABLE OF CONTENTS

TABLE OF CONTENTS
(Continued)

TABLE OF CONTENTS
(Continued)

FOREWORD

The idea of "developing" modern Africa has been a subject of intense controversy. Theoretically and philosophically, some have argued that Africa, the "cradle of human civilization," should not be obsessed with "development and modernization" simply because some imperialists and colonizers successfully conspired to do havoc to Africa by "underdeveloping" the continent. According to these people, the pursuit of modernization and development, as these terms apply to Africa in theory and in practice, is playing a "Western" game, by Western rules, and in competition with the West; "a game system that not only gives Africa no chance of winning but also promises to make Africa even more of a marginal observer in the "Super Bowl of World History."

The basic problem, however, is that some irreversible changes in the world economic, technological, political, and even cultural environments have made it impossible for anybody to say for sure, if, and to what degree any country or region of the world can set its own rules for the economic, technological, political, and cultural world games. Because communication and its technology have become central elements in these games, one of the most advisable courses of action for Africa to take is to assess the place of the continent's communication and technology resources as an aspect of the infrastructure for the past and present socioeconomic challenges and successes in the continent and as a guide as to how best to organize for a better and more competitive future.

Dr. Riverson's book, *Telecommunications Development: The Case of Africa,* focuses on the issue of how Africa is, and should be, organizing itself for the optimal use of its telecommunications resources for economic development. Dr. Riverson has provided us with much needed information on where modern Africa has been, where it is, and where it should be going in order to avoid the sector and regional malintegration that has been the bane of telecommunications effectiveness in Africa. The book is necessary reading for all those who want to understand the challenge of the institutional relationship between telecommunications and development in modern Africa.

Dr. R. Nwafo Nwanko
Graduate Professor
Howard University
Washington, D.C.

PREFACE

"Education's purpose is to replace an empty mind with an open one."

Malcom S. Forbes

One of the main frustrations that turned out to be an encouragement for me to write this book is the difficulty I encountered when searching for literature on African telecommunications development. The lack of proper documentation and distribution of information is a shameful situation in Africa. The Africans themselves turn to the developed nations for information about their own countries. To see myself not as part of this problem but part of the solution, I decided to write this book.

It is true that Africa is old, but it does not stop her in becoming developed. Africa lags behind all the other regions of the world in "development." And this contributes to my belief that "if trade is the lifeblood of an economy, then telecommunications systems can truly be regarded as the nerve system of both the economy and society."

Telecommunications, including computers, are tools that will make work easier and productive, as well as bring total development to the African society. If only Africans recognized that "Information is Power."

I take this opportunity to say "Wake-up Africa," — develop your telecommunications infrastructure, and all your education, health, transportation, industries, and other developmental sector problems will be resolved.

This book's primary objective is to examine the development of telecommunications in Africa. I explain how telecommunications affect economic development. Specifically, in the case of Africa, the Pan-African Telecommunications Network (PANAFTEL) is analyzed *vis-à-vis* its infrastructural programs to support the goals and objectives of the African economic development plan. My analysis was shaped by questions concerning the current state of African telecommunications development, the priority ranking on the agendas of African countries for telecommunications development, and the need to assess the role of PANAFTEL provision of telecommunications services designed to meet the defined African economic objectives.

This book traces the historical development of the Pan-African Telecommunications Network including four of its subregional networks: PANAFTEL-North, PANAFTEL-West (ECOWAS-Network), PANAFTEL-Central, and PANAFTEL-South (SADCC-Network). For each subregion there is a descriptive analysis of the infrastructure, technology, operation, and other associated development factors.

On the future of telecommunications development in Africa, I shed light on the emergence of the Regional African Satellite Communication System (RASCOM) which could revolutionize African telecommunications. Also, I made a number of recommendations on aiding African telecommunications development. Together with other experts on African telecommunications, we will continue to contribute our resources to the development of Africa as a whole.

CHAPTER I
Introduction

According to the World Bank, telecommunications networks may be described as the central nervous system of complex societies, transmitting information and commands among the various parts of such societies. Without these facilities, many activities in inter-related sectors of society, especially government and economic activities, could not function efficiently. Modern telecommunications encompass services and facilities for transmission of written messages, voice communication modes such as television and radio, data and facsimile, satellite, and terrestrial telemetering and microwave applications. These technological services provide telephone, telegraph, telex, audio, video, and other facilities to the public to meet a variety of needs that make life easier and that improve the human condition.

One of the major prerequisites of economic integration in a modern and complex society is the development of a sound infrastructure in the telecommunications sector. The establishment of a modern, reliable, and rapidly expanding telecommunications network contributes considerably to the promotion of a variety of activities of economic expansion.[1] The African continent, three-and-a-half times the size of the United States of America, consists of some fifty-four countries. It is within this complex geographical framework that the Organization of African Unity (OAU) and the Economic Commission for Africa (ECA) recognized the urgent need to develop an inter-African telecommunications network while preserving the continent's commercial and cultural links with the other parts of the world. It was, nevertheless, the recognition of the need for an African continent-wide telecommunications network that laid a basis for the Pan-African Telecommunications Network.[2] In 1987, for instance, Ivorian President Felix Houphouet Boigny warned his country's citizens that "Africa missed the industrial revolution; we can't afford to stand aside and let the communication revolution go by, too."[3] This statement implies that telecommunications development is a vital need of the entire continent. It is understood, however, that the living conditions of African societies are affected by forces outside of the telecommunications arena.

PANAFTEL is the acronym for the Pan-African Telecommunication Network, which was formed by the interconnection of the telecommunications systems of fifty African nations. The only viable Pan-African telecommunications network, PANAFTEL has facilities that include transmission links, microwave facilities, submarine cable facilities, domestic and international switching facilities, domestic and international telex exchange facilities, and supplementary satellite communication earth stations. The development of the PANAFTEL network is at the advanced development and implementation stages. The network currently provides telephone, telex, television, and radio signals to and from all the African nations. These accomplishments were made possible through the efforts put forth by the OAU and the individual African governments. PANAFTEL is coordinated and assisted by the International Telecommunication Union (ITU) and the ECA, supported by the United Nations Development Program (UNDP), with funding from several multilateral and bilateral financing institutions.

In the past, the African telecommunications networks were dominated by commercial administrative relations with Europe and other parts of the Western world. As a consequence, most of the domestic traffic continues to be routed through Europe and other foreign satellites, a situation that makes the provision of services expensive.[4] Each of the fifty sovereign independent African member states is responsible for developing its own national telecommunications system that links with a sub-regional network. The four sub-regional networks are known as the Economic Community of West African States (ECOWAS) network, the Middle East and Mediterranean Arab States Network-link (MEDARABTEL), the African Conference of Central African Post and Telecommunications (CAPTAC), and the Southern African Telecommunications Network (SATCO). They are now parts of the overall infrastructure of PANAFTEL. The development of telecommunications has been a fast-paced process and has become an unanticipated political and economic issue in almost all African countries in recent years. The new technologies that PANAFTEL provides are changing every phase of information development and erasing boundaries that have separated the African nations.[5]

In mapping the future of African development, Lauffer (1984) has asked whether these technologies, if carefully planned, implemented, and applied, can help Africa speed up the economic development process to any significant degree, or whether they will set back Africa's development. The new technologies have many implications. For example, many of them require fewer workers than traditional technologies; and those few must be highly skilled. In addition, technological changes could mean the demand for different levels of jobs with vast differences in training requirements. These changes may also require that the limited supply of trained manpower be allocated to help advance the growth of the whole African continent.

Although the future of Africa's communication and information system is not yet clear, it is being pursued on a number of fronts. The planning and implementation of PANAFTEL is one of these fronts. It is in this context of need that this book was written. This book traces the history of telecommunications development in Africa with a view to describing its technologies, operations, and associated factors. It is expected that this effort would be helpful in determining the current status of PANAFTEL in the African economic development agenda and its potential role in the socioeconomic development of Africa. This book, thus, focuses on the following issues:

1. telecommunications developments that have occurred and are occurring in Africa;
2. the major factors that have affected PANAFTEL development;
3. the status of PANAFTEL in the economic development agenda of Africa;
4. the potential role of PANAFTEL in the socioeconomic development of Africa.

PANAFTEL, an interconnection of the telecommunications systems of fifty African nations, is coordinated by the individual African governments, the Organization of African Unity (OAU), the International Telecommunication Union (ITU), and the Economic Commission for Africa (ECA). It is supported by the United Nations Development Program (UNDP), with funding from multilateral and bilateral financing institutions. PANAFTEL is a unique institution in Africa in that it is the only inter-African network that includes every African country as a participant.

As of today, not a single book has focused directly on African telecommunications. Partial information concerning telecommunications services in Africa has addressed such issues as: one, the African countries' involvement in the international telecommunications sphere; two, the evolution of telecommunications needs in one specific African country; three, the development of the African telecommunications market; and four, the distribution of the space spectrum in selected member countries of the ITU. Cultural diversity and the disparities in the levels of development among African countries pose serious challenges to policy makers who are responsible for mapping the future direction of African telecommunications. This book provides a comprehensive picture of the development of telecommunications in Africa, including its current technologies, with a view to furnishing guideposts for future planning and policymaking.

It is the purpose of this book to examine PANAFTEL development from its inception to the present, including its technologies and operations with the view of providing some guidelines for use by African policymakers. The focus of the investigation was shaped by questions about the background and current status of PANAFTEL, setbacks in PANAFTEL implementation, the placement of PANAFTEL's development on the priority agenda for Africa's economic development effort, and the potential contribution of PANAFTEL to the objectives of African development. The design of the study assumes that a comprehensive picture of PANAFTEL's development is useful as a basis for future planning of development projects in Africa.

DEFINITION OF TERMS

TELECOMMUNICATIONS: All types of communication systems in which electric or electromagnetic signals are used to transmit information between or among points. Transmission media may be radio, light, or waves in other portions of the electromagnetic spectrum, such as cable, satellite, microwave, or any other medium.

NETWORK: An interconnected system of transmission lines that provides multiple connections among different locations.

SYSTEM: An assembly of component parts linked together by some form of regulated interaction into an organized whole.

INFRASTRUCTURE: The subordinate parts, installations, or establishments that form the basis of an enterprise.

DEVELOPMENT: A process of growth, advancement, etc. that improves the human living condition.

ANTENNA: A device used to pick up on-air audio and video signals.

COMMUNICATION SATELLITE: An orbiting space vehicle that actively or passively relays signals between communications stations.

EARTH STATION: Equipment located on earth used for the transmission and/or reception of signals to a communication satellite.

FREQUENCY: The number of waves of electrical energy sent out each second, usually expressed in cycles per second, or hertz (Hz).

MICROWAVE: Method of transmitting signals over the air from an origination point to receivers in line-of-sight at high frequency.

AUTOMATIC SWITCHING EQUIPMENT: That part of an exchange in a switched system which routes calls automatically to make the connections requested by calling parties.

CROSSBAR EXCHANGE: An exchange in which a bar rotated by a solenoid is used to make switched connections between circuits to connect incoming calls to outgoing calls.

ELECTRONIC EXCHANGE: An electronic exchange is a telephone exchange which uses electronic switching components rather than electromechanical components.

TELEPHONE: Public switched telephone network which is a system for transmitting voice signals in the audio frequency range over a network servicing a very large user population.

TELEGRAPH (TELEX): Widely used international service, which is based on the transmission and reception of printed messages using teletypewriters as subscriber terminals.

This section develops the framework of this book. It discusses how information in this book was obtained and organized in relation to the major dimensions of the scholarly approach. The scope of the study called for examining the history of telecommunications development of Africa and identifying its technologies and operations, with special reference to the economic agenda of the whole African region.

Two assumptions provided the orientation for this book. The first was that no change is a singular event but is, instead, a function of the inter-relatedness of several forces and factors. Accordingly, an interactive approach to telecommunications development was considered useful in obtaining a representative set of the contingencies in the African economic sphere. The other assumption was that a longitudinal or historical view of African telecommunications development would enhance our understanding of the pace of adaptation of these new technologies.

In accepting these assumptions, it was necessary to use procedures that would yield a comprehensive picture of the development of telecommunications, with a view to deriving generalization that could be applied in other projects involving Africa's development. A review and analysis of the literature and other existing data would effectively serve the requirements of the investigation, especially given the nature and availability of critical materials, the dearth of reports of research that were closely related to the present study, and the complexity of the data sought. Other data collection techniques such as field studies, experimentation, person-to-person interviews, and written surveys were not feasible for this investigation. Protocol clearance requirements and other security measures, as well as language barriers and cost limitation factors inherent in these alternatives, influenced the choice of the literature and existing data search as the major approach.

This book has, therefore, taken into account these overriding concerns and will describe African telecommunications development in the context of its broader scope to provide evidence of:

1. telecommunications developments that have occurred and are occurring in Africa;
2. the major factors that have affected PANAFTEL development;
3. the status of PANAFTEL's development in the economic agenda of the four sub-regional groups; and
4. the potential contribution of the PANAFTEL network to the objective of the African economic development effort.

This book is also a reaction to the "New Communication Order"[6] which campaigned for the use of communications in national development.

SOURCES OF INFORMATION

The data that were pertinent to developing the historical analysis of African telecommunications development and operations were obtained from materials published by the following resource centers: ITU, ECA, United Nations Education Scientific and Cultural Affairs (UNESCO), International

Telecommunications Satellite Organization (INTELSAT), Agency for International Development (AID), Academy for Educational Development (AED), and the World Bank.

The following criteria were used in selecting the data sources: scope of information, depth of coverage, availability of materials, and recency of content. These data consisted of reports from committees, seminars, conferences, proceedings, position papers, and other documents such as annual reports and technical journals. The materials related to African telecommunications development. The current operation and technologies of PANAFTEL were profiled in a general summary and then described in detail under the headings of the PANAFTEL's four subregional networks identified as: PANAFTEL-North, PANAFTEL-West, PANAFTEL-Central, and PANAFTEL-South.

CHAPTER I

NOTES

1. World Bank. *Telecommunication Sector Working Paper*. Washington, D. C.: World Bank, 1971.

2. International Telecommunications Union. *Pan-African Telecommunications Network*. Geneva, Switzerland: ITU, 1983, 1986 and 1987.

3. "PANAFTEL-West: Bringing microwave to Africa." *African Telecommunications Report*. 1(12), 1987.

4. International Telecommunications Union. Pan-African Telecommunications Network Publication. International Telecommunications Union, Geneva: ITU, 1972, 1981, 1983, and 1987.

5. Lauffer, S. "Policy considerations." *Development Communication Report*, Washington, D.C.: A.E.D., 1984.

6. Till, D. *World Communication Year. New Communication Order*, 8, 9, 10, UNESCO: Communication Documentation Center. Paris: 1983.

CHAPTER II
Telecommunications
and
Development

This chapter presents a review of the literature directly related to telecommunications development in Africa. It first presents the background to the second conference on African Telecommunication Administration and its PANAFTEL resolutions. Then, it discusses the role of telecommunications in development and the major factors constraining the development and application of telecommunications facilities.

Anasiudu has surveyed how African countries utilize the INTELSAT facilities for domestic, intra-African, and inter-continental telecommunications.[1] The evidence shows that, as a result of the unequal distribution of wealth and technological resources among African nations, a lopsided development exists in INTELSAT whereby the technological spin-off benefits which are open to INTELSAT members are skewed in favor of a few advanced member nations. This situation, he points out, has left African signatories and other less developed countries in the position of clients making use of the available facilities but benefiting little from INTELSAT's impact on the technical and industrial area. Anasiudu also noted that the colonialists did not cater to telecommunications development in the interest of the African nations during the early stages of the ITU development. In the struggle to control or resist a worldwide monopoly of wireless telegraphy by one individual nation, the colonialists overlooked the possibility of their African colonies gaining independence in the future. Anasiudu further asserts that insofar as the whole satellite communications field has brought the technologically weak countries to a level of technological dependence on a few outside production and distribution centers, it has presented both advantages and disadvantages.

In responding to Anasiudu's argument, Udofia documents frequency allocations, radio regulations, and proceedings of nine selected ITU conferences between 1903 and 1979.[2] The findings present the comparisons of frequencies that were allocated to the developed and African countries during the 1903 inaugural radio conference at Berlin. Udofia also analyzed the advantages and disadvantages of African countries' participation in INTELSAT and assessed the political, economic, cultural, and social ramifications of imminent direct television transmission for satellite (DTTS) for African countries.

Oziri's work examined the evolution of telecommunications needs in Nigeria, and made a needs analysis regarding future telecommunications development and strategies of African communications. His findings support the claims that no nation can be cohesive where one part is highly literate or informed and the other is uninformed. Oziri recommends that the "reach" of broadcasting must be expanded by providing low-cost receivers to every African village. With satellite services available, all African nations should be able to bring television to most parts of their territories to help in national development efforts.[3]

Sy's research presents a detailed comparative analysis of the evolution of the African telecommunications market during the post-colonial period, in relation to the colonial legacy and the new demands born out of the total integration of the national telecommunications networks in the international telecommunications market placed under the control of Western imperialism. In addition, he presents the present and future telecommunications policies carried out in Africa by the ITU, INTELSAT, and the World Bank.[4]

The contributions of Anasiudu, Udofia, and Sy have emphasized some of the fundamental issues concerning telecommunications development in Africa and its relations to global systems and forces.

CONCEPTUAL FRAMEWORK

The brief review above suggests that telecommunications are essential to economic development, and the purpose of the conceptual framework here is an attempt to give PANAFTEL development a central role in the African and global development and modernization process. This book is, therefore, guided by Lerner's dominant communications development and modernization paradigm, which has spurred various research works that have become grounds for academic and intellectual debate. Lerner argues that the Western communications and development model exhibits certain components and sequences whose relevance is global. The Western model, according to Lerner, is considered to be a general developmental model which is virtually an inevitable baseline for development planning because there is no other model which can serve this purpose.[5]

Lerner also explores the dichotomy between the traditional and modern structure of society in terms of their influences and their relation to development. In so doing, he suggests in *The Passing of Traditional Society* the inevitability of a historical process. When development occurs by natural laws, policy has to adjust, for there is no point in moving against the tide of such global processes of developments.

"Modernization" for Lerner is, thus, merely a new name for an old process:

" . . . the process of social change whereby less-developed societies acquire characteristics common to more developed societies."

Underlying Lerner's thesis is a convergence theory:

"It has been said that through acculturation — the taking over of a foreign culture or some of its elements — a kind of universal standardization of the human being would result."[6]

PANAFTEL development put the African society into a challenging position. One can dismiss neither the arguments for African cultural conservation nor the Western idea of freedom of information. The new information technologies, however, favor diversity and openness. African governments, according to Stover, usually react to fear of change and cultural invasion, while other nations or societies continue to seek economic prosperity.[7] This would suggest that within the economic realm, human beings who act rationally will proliferate over the entire globe. The proliferation of industrialization, accordingly, would mean the diffusion of specific cultural traits.[8]

The thesis that modernization is a worldwide process is also supported by Parsons. In *The Systems of Modern Societies*, Parsons stated that "the trend toward modernization has become worldwide, which denotes a cluster of social processes such as the taking over of scientifically-based technologies, the proliferation of a state-sponsored system of urbanizaiton, secularization, increasing interdependence within the society, and the introduction of mass communication."[9] Within this cluster, a problematic aspect is that modernization processes can proceed variously in different sectors (e.g., the technological, political, economic, and informational sectors), a fact that makes operations within a research frame considerably more difficult.

Rapid technological change brings an expanding awareness and renewed attention to any field of endeavor. In a sense, the study of society's evolution has traced the uncertain footsteps of changing technology down uncharted paths of economic development. In communications, the modern society is on the brink of an interacting series of technological changes of a magnitude that will virtually dwarf all past changes. The impact of the new communications technologies in the economic, political, social, and cultural sectors is enormous, but it is not clear whether their net effects will be optimal or even beneficial in satisfying human needs, or whether society might prefer to pursue a different course if it were aware of and could select from alternative paths.[10]

Despite the realism of this argument, Rao postulates that global communication systems can provide forces for cohesion or instruments of cultural invasion: "The science of communication, the study of the communication process, the expanding field of the mass communication theory and the 'instant technology' of electronic communications are still as dazzlingly modern or suspiciously futuristic—depending on whether it is seen as one of the contemporary phenomena enriching our lives or just another aspect of the modern technological-cultural syndrome."[11]

Telecommunications, mass communication, and other information technologies can effect change in developing countries, but the leaders are often disappointed in the results, according to Stover, because when these countries acquire the physical means of communication, those same leaders attempt to control communications, resulting in forms of censorship that prevent genuine communication. Stover looked closely at information technology and communication as agents of economic, social, and political development in developing countries, stressing that definitions of "communication" and "development" must include participation in the exchange of information and the attainment of humane values.

There is no question that Africa needs a modern telecommunications network like PANAFTEL to facilitate her capacity to reshape world trade, international business, agricultural production, and food security and to cope more effectively with crises such as extreme weather conditions, crop failures, and epidemics. O'Brien asserts that after the adaptation of these technologies, the impact cannot be immediately observed but can, nevertheless, have far-reaching consequences. Exposure to foreign technologies can suggest new ideas of self-identity and patterns of behavior for children, teenagers, women, men, students, workers, housewives, businessmen, executives, and even policymakers. Therefore, the rich, old African traditional values could be at stake and may have to accommodate a new value system or give way to electronic colonization.[12]

By analyzing this transition, Fisher explained that what the world is observing is a large-scale acculturation process taking place in human history, and communication is the essence of its momentum.[13] This is where the idea of developing a "global society" is analytically fruitful, for it is within this large context that these social and cultural movements make the most sense. Mass communication, in particular, is designed to create, animate, and influence human society.[14]

Despite the glitter, promise or threats, and implications of the new communications technologies, nothing is so important as their consequences upon everyone's daily lives, Williams stresses.[15] These consequences do not tend to be entirely new activities, but rather appear more as change in traditional services and the institutions which supply them. It is in this context that the analysis of the history and current operation of PANAFTEL is relevant.

Most of the research works on the development of PANAFTEL address the common fundamental objective established during the second conference on African Telecommunications Administration, held in Kinshasa in December 1979. The basic objective of the members was to mobilize all their forces through:

- Development of telecommunications to achieve unity. PANAF-TEL has adopted sixteen resolutions in support of achieving its basic objective. Because the greatest development problem Africa faces is the lack of a technically trained labor force, six of these resolutions concentrated on manpower training.

- Other development problems dealt with in the adopted resolutions were a pre-investment survey; the use of the PANAFTEL network; coordination meetings at the West African sub-regional level; rural telecommunications requirements; rates and tariffs; development of national networks; satellite systems; operational maintenance; establishment of training centers for instructors; manpower development; and broadcast and television training.

Perhaps none of these resolutions can stand alone as being the most important because it is the "sum of the whole" that makes PANAFTEL a reality. However, two resolutions merit further elaboration in the study.

RESOLUTION NO. 1:
THE ESTABLISHMENT OF PANAFTEL

The striking aspects of the background to Resolution No. 1 are explicit and are quoted because of their relevance to the present study:

CONSCIOUS of the need to ensure orderly development of regional telecommunications services at a pace commensurate with the political, economic, and social development of Africa.

CONSIDERING that there is a need arising out of the current development of Pan-African telecommunications for collective action the detailed planning and management of the projected regional telecommunication network.

CONVINCED of the need for a Pan-African organization making possible the coordination of telecommunications development policies in Africa and the harmonization of operational arrangements among the National Telecommunications Administrations of the continent.

RESOLUTION NO. 5:
COORDINATION OF TELECOMMUNICATIONS DEVELOPMENT

With the technical data provided by the ITU to PANAFTEL, it was recognized by the African Telecommunications Administrators that the regional effort was grandiose, that extensive coordination would be required on a continental and subcontinental basis. Therefore, Resolution No. 5 recommends:

That administrations hold subregional coordination meetings at least once a year to consider all technical, administrative, and financial issues relating to the implementation of the PANAFTEL network; that the regional advisors on telecommunications should continue to give assistance in the subregional coordination of the PANAFTEL project.[16]

THE ROLE OF TELECOMMUNICATIONS IN A DEVELOPING ECONOMY

There are few studies which can give a scientific explanation of the impact of telecommunications on economic growth. It has, however, become essential that African countries be presented with evidence of the importance of telecommunications—especially telephone, telex, radio, and TV — for their economic growth. The greater the shortage of foreign currency in most African countries, the more difficult it is for their governments to select priorities. The readily available means will be devoted, in the first place, to meeting prime necessities, such as food and medical care. Any further funds will have to be divided among needs such as education, transport, and telecommunications. In this distribution, the means allocated to ministries of telecommunications are invariably inadequate. In addition, investments in this field are relatively expensive.

The subject was debated at the International Telecommunications Union Plenipotentiary Conference in Nairobi in 1982. One of the conclusions reached was that African ministries needed arguments which could help them prove the economic usefulness of telephone links. The ITU, in an attempt to provide such arguments, has studied the situation in African countries. It has come to the conclusion that qualitative arguments are not enough, and that a plea in favor of telecommunications can only succeed if it is quantified.

The first clear fact to emerge from ITU's study was the uneven distribution of telephone densities, which in African countries are on average ten times higher in towns than in rural areas. Although the towns are usually relatively prosperous, African countries often geographically cover vast territories which are predominantly rural. Telephone investments and maintenance in urban areas are relatively cheap, owing to the short distance between telephones. The reverse is true, however, in the rural areas, where telephones are expensive to install. It may be more effective, therefore, to lay greater emphasis on justifying the need for telephones in rural areas, and on demonstrating that this need is greater in rural areas than elsewhere.

The economic benefit of the telephone for the user may be twice as much as he/she has to pay for the call; for example, he/she may be able to avoid a journey. It may be assumed that if a low income earner decides to devote such a considerable sum to a telephone call, it must be because he/she is strongly motivated. Most African countries have satisfactory land communications. The telephone would be used, therefore, only in calls where the alternative journey is either prohibitively expensive or would not achieve the desired objective. This situation may arise for a user once or twice a year, according to ITU 1987 estimates.[17]

Based on another economic analysis, the telephone can provide other benefits to businesses. In industrialized countries, however, a business cannot operate without a telephone. This situation is not the case in most African countries, where, with the prevailing socioeconomic structure, the size of villages, and the existence of a market, it is possible to do business without a telephone. Once there is a degree of economic specialization in particular regions or businesses, however, rapid telecommunications become indispensable. Conversely, the installation of a telephone infrastructure can bring about modifications in the economic structure by enabling businesses working in specialized fields to survive, giving them a broader coverage of customers and geographical areas.

Such a convincing economic argument, however, does not take certain qualitative factors into account because qualitative considerations depend on values which can be controversial. With reference to the issue of national unity as an example, the economic value — in this case the telephone — may be a double-edged instrument. It can be used by rebels as well as by government authorities. Telexes may be intercepted and read by people for whom they were not intended. Telecommunications may therefore be considered a threat by certain African regimes.[18]

ECONOMIC DEVELOPMENT AND SOCIAL CHANGE

Telecommunications system will allow rural populations access to price or market information which may promote a more efficient marketing and distribution system, whether by radio, television, or telephone. The access to specialized expertise increases efficiency in production.[19] In general, it is possible that access to a two-way, instantaneous transmission telecommunications network could increase productivity of various types of economic enterprises by speeding the run around times for ordering and production, allowing specific information input to be drawn upon as needed during the production process, and matching production more closely to changes in market demand.

Many organizations have recognized the developmental value or indirect benefits of telecommunications. The World Bank stated the following in 1971:

"The value of telecommunications services to users is attested to by the unsatisfied demand throughout the developing world, even at prices which generate very substantial surpluses for reinvestment and thus probably capture a much larger share of user benefits than in any other public service."[20]

In one of his papers, Dickenson of the World Bank states:

"If trade is the lifeblood of an economy, then telecommunications can truly be regarded as the nervous system of both the economy and society."[21]

It has been noted by experts in the field that telecommunications development in rural areas may help counteract the rural exodus to the towns, which is a serious problem in many African countries. Rural telecommunications development may allow a more balanced development of a nation by allowing business and government agencies to operate outside the large urban areas. The introduction of telecommunications services in a region can alter considerably its patterns of communication. Wellenius finds that three types of phenomena take place:

- substitution for alternative means (such as transportation, mail, and telegraph);
- creation of a new communication medium which would not have developed with telecommunications;
- new requirements on other communications (e.g., transportation) as a consequence of the increase in intensity of interaction.[22]

The existence of a telecommunications system may be necessary to support the new types of organizations which occur as part of the development process. Cherry has observed that "in the economic sphere, the telephone service is essentially organizational in function; it creates productive traffic."[23]

Parker has observed that telecommunications may both reflect and reinforce the social structure of a nation. Parker views institutional structures as composed of communication patterns which may be shaped by the communications technology available to society:

> "The communication technology of a society determines who can speak to whom, over what distances, with what time delays, and with what possibilities for feedback or return communication. This is the heart of what is meant by social organization. It makes less sense to say that the social organization is caused by the pattern of communication interactions in the society than it does to define the social structure in terms of the patterns of communication (including order-giving). The culture of a society can be defined by the messages of a society that are transmitted in these social patterns. The messages of a society are obviously shaped by the media they are transmitted through, as well as being creations of the institutional structure of society. Therefore, careful attention should be paid to the form of the communication technology installed in support of the development."[24]

It is important to note that the existence of a telephone channel does not cause social change, but rather allows it to proceed.

TELECOMMUNICATIONS AS AN ESSENTIAL COMMODITY

While the overall findings about the relation of telecommunications and rural development are somewhat inconclusive, they all suggest one important element: the effects of telephone investment do not accrue to individual users, but to society in general, and rural society in particular. Although the 'good' which is sold may be defined as the individual telephone call or as access to the telephone network, the social benefits in terms of improved health, productivity, education, and the like may accrue to those who do not directly use the telephone. As such, attempts to treat the good as a *private* good may lead to underinvestment or underconsumption of the *public* good.

The difference between an investment and a pricing approach based on "telephone as a public good" versus "telephone as a private good" is significant especially in terms of rural telephone service. Treating telephone service as purely a commercial good necessarily leads to investment policies that favor urban areas and leave rural areas under served. The reason underlying these development shifts is that the high densities of population and relatively high incomes are less expensive to serve and produce higher direct returns to capital than do rural areas. However, if the criterion of public goods is used, it is possible that the benefits arising from telephone service, in terms of economic and social development, may justify the investment in telephone service — even though the direct returns on capital will be low.[25]

TELECOMMUNICATIONS IMPROVES RURAL SOCIAL SERVICES

In countries where a political and economic commitment has been made to provide rural social services (e.g., health care, education, agricultural extension services) a key policy question concerns the cost-effectiveness of the alternate ways of providing the services. Locating highly or moderately trained professional or para-professional workers in rural locations may not be feasible because of the high initial training costs, the continuing salary costs, and the bureaucratic overhead costs (including communication and transportation) of managing a large, geographically dispersed organization. Even if a sufficient number of highly trained personnel were available and budgets were sufficient to pay their salaries, it still might be very difficult to induce them to live and work in rural locations.[26] If minimally trained rural workers are utilized on either a volunteer or nominally paid basis, then the requirements of management, supervision, and continuing education would be greatly increased.

In the absence of a good telecommunications infrastructure, the travel and professional labor costs associated with management, supervision, and continuing education may be prohibitively expensive. But without them, the program may be significantly less effective. The consequences may be a lower quality of rural education, the unavailability of agricultural extension information to subsistence farmers, and poor or non-existent rural health care. With reliable rural telecommunications, telephony or audio conference circuits may be used to provide supervision and assistance to rural workers. Instructional radio programs may be delivered electronically to rural schools and supervised by partially-trained teachers or education aides. Timely feedback from the schools to project managers would be essential to the success of such projects. Rural health workers who are unable to consult with nurses and physicians affiliated with district hospitals or clinics would, consequently, be able to provide better local health care. These kinds of applications may be possible only in locations with reliable telecommunications.

The prevailing economic theory concludes that the optimal allocation of economic resources occurs when the two conditions of perfect competition and perfect information are met. In socialist economies, the availability of information is even more important for the efficient allocation of resources because the flow of money does not constitute the same signal that it does in a competitive economy. Rural areas that lack a telecommunications infrastructure are thus at an information disadvantage (and consequently an economic disadvantage) relative to the urban areas which have both more developed telecommunications and lower cost transportation substitutes.

In rural agriculture, the timely access to relevant information such as weather reports and prices and the availability of necessary inputs (seeds, fertilizer, tools, credit, etc.) should make rural agricultural enterprise more efficient. The timely access to technical agricultural information, such as might be provided by an agricultural extension service, may also make agriculture more efficient.

In African countries rural population growth has led to a surplus of labor relative to the available agricultural land. If land were all redistributed 'equitably,' the resulting plots might be too small to be economically viable. Rural-urban migration patterns are putting great pressure on urban areas with insufficient jobs and insufficient urban services and infrastructure (e.g., water and sewage systems). Consequently, the development of rural non-farm enterprises may be a necessary part of national economic development plans. The availability of an underemployed rural labor force (at advantageous wage rates) for whom new urban housing need not be provided, may provide an incentive for rural enterprise — if reliable telecommunications and transportation infrastructures are available to facilitate the coordination of the necessary inputs and marketing activities.

African governments and multilateral and bilateral development programs are insisting on greater social equity as a development goal, including the provision of services aimed at helping people in rural areas. In a direct way, the provision of a rural component in national telecommunications development plans would meet this objective.

More important, perhaps, than the direct benefits of rural telecommunications (e.g., jobs in installation, operation, and maintenance) are the indirect consequences for the distribution of economic benefits. The improved cost-effectiveness of social service delivery programs and facilitation of increased or more productive economic activity, as discussed above, would contribute to this goal of reduced inequity.

In addition, the availability of reliable telecommunications linking rural to urban areas may make it easier for people in rural areas to make their needs and wishes known. As a result, rural people may be able to be more effective in claiming their fair share of national budgets. To the extent that government bureaucracies that operate on the principle that a telecommunications infrastructure will enable them to hear the views of rural people, then such an infrastructure may be beneficial to them.

Cherry refers to telecommunications services (telephone, telex, telegram) as organizational media (as opposed to the 'informational' mass media). In developing countries, the assumption should not be made that people will spontaneously begin to use the telephone to gather information or to form organizational linkages. However, it is possible that the telephone could be used for organizational and informational purposes within the existing institutional framework. An institutional framework exists in all types of societies: a traditional village with chiefs, elders, or counselors; a commune; or an urban collectivity of families with strong neighborhood or cultural ties. They need not be a preoccupation with indicators of 'modernization' but rather of organization or functional networks.

One can expect that communication will begin within these networks:

- among members of extended families;

- between tiers of workers in a service organization, such as a health system;

- between field staff and administrative staff in development projects.

As the scope of interest broadens and communities of interest widen, the telephone system will reinforce new linkages, for example, between leaders within a region and between local representatives and central officials.

In Africa, there is no denial that telecommunications have played an important role in raising productivity and promoting the diversification of economic activities, as well as being the media for the exchange and rapid dissemination of information. Telecommunications are confirmed means of mass education; they have enabled the rapid transmission of instruction, advice, and feedback in decentralized organizations. They have been essential aids for relief programs during disasters. They have made it possible for remote medical consultations and health care. They have been factors in the rural-urban migration. They have contributed to the development and cultural exchange. And they have been a major contributing factor to national unity, understanding, and political stability. Telecommunications have therefore contributed to the economic growth and the raising of the quality of life in Africa.

Twenty-six African countries are considered to be among the Least Developed Countries (LDCs). Africa also has the lowest average Direct Exchange Lines (DELs), or main lines, density among the developing countries; the 1980 figures show 0.5 DELs to 100 inhabitants in Africa, compared with 5.7 for Latin America, and 5.8 for Asia. It is of interest to note that the world average was then 19 DELs per 100 people, that of industrialized countries, 44 per 100 people, and that of developing countries 3 per 100 people

The telephone penetration is even less in the rural and remote areas of Africa where about 80 percent of the population live. It is in the light of these disparities, among others, that the United Nations General Assembly had earlier proclaimed 1978 to 1988 as the United Nations Transportation and Communications Decade for Africa (UNTACDA) with the principal goals being independence, self-reliance, and international cooperation among the African states in the field of transport and communications. Among its objectives, UNTACDA called for an end of decade telephone density of 1.0 per 100 inhabitants and one Public Call Office (PCO) per 10,000 rural population, distributed such that each inhabitant might live within five km of a telephone. Based on the low growth rate and other shortcomings in development policies, the heads of state and government of the OAU included transport and communications among the five priority sectors of its Lagos Plan of Action and Final Act of Lagos in 1980. They established the achievement of the UNTACDA telephone density targets by the year 2000, through the implementation of the PANAFTEL, as a top priority. The 1984 estimate of telephone density in Africa is 0.68 DELs per 100 people.[27]

An assessment of the fundamental importance of communications infra-structures as an essential element in the economic and social development of all countries shows that the 1982 Plenipotentiary Conference of the ITU at Nairobi set up the Independent Commission for World-Wide Telecommunications Development to recommend ways to stimulate the expansion of telecommunications across the world. The Commission reported the following:

• SERVICES

In the areas like health, education, transport, and social services, telecom-munications services are essential for the improvement of direct contact and coordination, optimization of skills, minimization of time lag, reduction in vehicle depreciation and down-time, quick relief in emergencies, mass con-tact, mass education, and improvement of adult literacy, especially in the rural and remote areas. Telecommunications provide effective institutional coordi-nation, data acquisition, and transmission, as well as project implementation follow-ups. Indeed, there can be no development without a telecommunica-tions component.

• INFRASTRUCTURE

In road development and maintenance, port and rail services, civil aviation, national security and defense, water and power supplies, telecom-munications are essential tools.

• ENVIRONMENT

Telecommunications services are also essential for the protection of the environment and natural resources against bush fires, pollution and poaching, remote sensing and early warning systems, drought and desertification control.

• TRADE AND FINANCE

The improvement of distributive channels for domestic and intra- African trade and marketing has benefited from telecommunications facilities.

Telecommunications services are also essential for the security, opera-tion, and maximization of profits in banking transactions, data transmission, daily bank balances and checks, mobilization of resources, rural bank services and supplies, network expansion, and the establishment of financial markets.

• INDUSTRIALIZATION

The availability of telecommunications services will rectify the imbal-ances in the development and geographical setting of industries, including cottage industries, management, and production capabilities. Local manufacturing of goods would, in turn, increase employment avenues, add value to raw materials, and save hard currency for many African countries. The availability of telecommunications services facilitates the formulation of population policies, programs, and resettlements with a view to accelerating socio-economic development.

The importance of these and other actions to achieve adequate telecommunications development in all countries cannot be overstressed. As the members of the International Commission for the Study of Communication Problems (the MacBride Commission) stated in *Many Voices. One World*:

> "Communications has become a vital need for collective entities and communities. Societies as a whole cannot survive today if they are not properly informed. Self-reliance, cultural identity, freedom, independence, respect for human dignity, mutual aid, participation in the reshaping of the environment— these are some of the non-material aspirations which all seek through communication. But higher productivity, better crops, enhanced efficiency and competition, improved health, appropriate marketing conditions, proper use of irrigation facilities are also objectives— among many others—which cannot be achieved without adequate communication and the provision of needed data."[28]

- ## TELECOMMUNICATIONS, DEVELOPMENT, AND SOCIAL CHANGE

The growing status of telecommunications internationally is also attributable to a growing recognition of the importance of telecommunications in all aspects of a nation's development, including agriculture, education, transportation, health care, rural-urban migration, and national and international trade and commerce. The study on telecommunications and development released jointly by ITU and the Organization for Economic Co-operation and Development (OECD) highlights the fact that "investments in telecommunications entail very significant economic and social benefits and contribute…to identifiable increases in gross national product. These increases…are greatest in the countries and regions with the lowest incomes."

One indication of the awareness and concern of decision-makers regarding the importance of telecommunications was the United Nations General Assembly declaration of the year 1983 as "World Communications Year." The objectives of World Communications Year are, first, to provide the opportunity for all countries to undertake an in-depth review and analysis of their policies on communications development, and second, to facilitate the accelerated development of communications infrastructures:

"These basic objectives are fully in line with the current concerns of all senior government officials, irrespective of the degree of development of their communications infrastructures. In view of the ever-growing importance of telecommunications, of the variety of the systems involved, and of the size of the investment required, it is easy to understand the... need for (a concerted effort) felt by all those called upon to take crucial decisions with regard to infrastructure for communications — that key factor in the social, economic, and cultural development of nations."[29]

Telecommunications is the lifeblood of business. Today's business world is indeed confronted with a revolution in information technology. Computers spew forth data on a scale so massive that their daily output exceeds the entire written works of mankind in bygone eras. In fact, the volume of information carried on communication systems is estimated to double every five years, and it will soon begin to double every two years.

These technologies are altering the very fabric of our lives. People and capital are in motion in a way that mankind could scarcely have dreamed of half a century ago. Business transactions that once took weeks to complete are now conducted in a fraction of a second. Today, business depends on telecommunications as an integral part of its day-to-day operations, and as the avenue for development of new products for carriers, operators, and manufacturers. These, however, represent only the tip of the proverbial iceberg of how telecommuniations can contribute to business and society.[30]

The efforts that are being coordinated as part of World Communications Year in Africa have been designed to complement the activities undertaken during UNTACDA, 1978-1987, which was declared in recognition of the urgency of developing transportation and communication infrastructure in Africa.

Statistics reveal the severity of the communication problem, not only in Africa, but in other developing regions as well. In January 1977, there were 0.4 telephones per 100 in Africa, 4.5 per 100 in South America, and 5.2 per 100 in Asia. This stands in sharp contrast to the 70.7 telephones per 100 people in North America.

Expanding on that picture, in 1977 developing countries as a whole had an average of 1.1 telephones per 100 population, while developed countries had an average of 33 per 100. In 1982, three-fourths of the 550 million telephones in the world were in only eight countries, and three-fourths of the 560 million television sets were in only nine countries. In other words, developing countries have 70 percent of the world's population, 20 percent of the world's gross national product, and 7 percent of the world's telephones and televisions.

Not only do African countries have fewer telephones, they also have a strong imbalance in service that favors urban over rural areas. A survey of 27 African countries revealed that 53 percent of all telephones in those countries were in the capital city — this despite the fact that over 80 percent of the population typically resides in rural areas.

This urban-rural communications imbalance has far-reaching effects, not the least of which is the negative effect on national cohesion that results from what is in effect a dual urban-rural economy. An ITU analysis of telecommunications revealed that 90 percent of telephone service in developing countries is used by subscribers in industry, business, banking, transportation, and government. Lacking telephone service, rural areas increasingly also lack access to important service sectors. Until policymakers learn to integrate telecommunications into the national planning process, the imbalance and its negative impact on national development and national cohesion are likely to prevail.

A comparison of annual telephone capacity growth rates is also revealing: North America has an annual growth rate of 4.6 percent, Europe 8 percent, Latin America 10 percent, and Africa between 6.2 and 8 percent. In order to achieve the goal of one telephone per 100 people in sub-Saharan Africa, where the need for telecommunications development is most pressing, an annual growth rate on the order of 14 percent is required. Levels of investment in telecommunications in developing countries have historically been low, averaging 0.3 percent of the gross domestic product, which is less than half of the average annual percentage of investment in developed countries.

Developing countries share a common set of problems regarding telecommunications: a huge gap between supply and demand, a strong distribution imbalance favoring urban over rural areas, poor quality of service, a long waiting time for new service, and peak traffic demands that exceed network capacity.

The costs of developing communication infrastructure are obviously great, and the lack of adequate financial resources is one of the fundamental constraints to improving the communication services. The problem is apt to reside in a shortage of available foreign exchange. The foreign exchange requirements of a telecommunications investment program are substantial— between 50 and 60 percent of the total required investment—primarily because the bulk of the equipment must be imported. Most developing countries have a shortage of foreign exchange. It can be expected that improved telecommunications will reduce the foreign exchange requirements of other sectors, such as transportation.

The availability of local currency for telecommunications investment should not be a problem, as local telephone operating entities usually average at least a 15 percent annual rate of return in most developing countries. Telecommunications entities are often not free to control the use of telecommunications revenues. Most countries mandate that not only must telecommunications make a profit, but that profit must be turned over in large amounts to the government to meet the expenses of other sectors. Left to itself, the telecommunications entity could not only support itself but could subsidize rural service. As it is, rural service often is not provided for from the public treasury because it is not immediately and obviously profitable. Rural services have high costs (up to five times the cost for urban services) and low traffic volume. This situation is self-perpetuating; low demand begets high prices, which, in turn, beget low demand.

There are additional constraints to the improvement of telecommunications, particularly in rural areas of developing countries. Related to the financing problem is the fact that there is a dearth of strong evidence of both the direct and indirect benefits of telecommunications investment, so that investments cannot be adequately justified. The ITU, the OECD, the World Bank, the AID Rural Satellite Program, and other organizations have been conducting systematic research to identify and measure the benefits of investments in telecommunications so that the sector can gain a more competitive position in the allocation of scarce financial resources.

Finally, there is a series of internal institutional problems that must be considered as constraints to telecommunications development. Primary among these are the lack of financial and management autonomy of most operating companies and the fragmentation of responsibility for telecommunications with different operating entities holding responsibility for different services. Fragmentation leads to higher costs, prevents economies of scale, leads to too much variety in equipment purchased, and causes duplication of managerial functions in a climate of managerial shortages.

THE JUSTIFICATION AND BENEFIT OF RURAL TELECOMMUNICATION DEVELOPMENT

A great percentage of Africa's population depends on rural economic activity for its livelihood. The economic future of this sector will determine that of Africa. The rural areas exhibit relatively low population density, low levels of economic activity, an absence of reliable primary power supply, shortages of qualified personnel, and remoteness from centers of supply and decision-taking. These areas are also required to absorb those persons who do not find employment in the modern sector. Socioeconomic conditions are characterized by high rates of adult illiteracy, inadequate supplies of health and educational services, nutritional deficiencies, low levels of income, and significant poverty.

The rural sector is not isolated from the rest of the economy. While affected by the latter, it is of cardinal significance at the macro level.

Rural Africa's development is thus integral to progress for the whole continent. The agricultural sector's contribution to Gross Domestic Product (GDP) typically sits around 35 percent and is even higher in most low-income economies. Non-farm activities boost the rural sector contribution to even higher levels. An important component of economic growth thus directly depends on rural output. Other facets are of equal importance. The export share of GDP is high, and the bulk of these foreign exchange earnings, which are crucial for import payment and industrial development, derive from primary products which largely depend (often in excess of 90 percent) on rural output. Government revenues, urban food supply and the balance of payments position are thus fundamentally influenced by the fate of the rural economy.[31]

RURAL TELECOMMUNICATIONS CONTRIBUTION TO DEVELOPMENT

Telecommunications play a vital part in fostering economy-wide development. The relationship of telephone density to GDP is well understood, and the causal importance of rural telecommunications in sectoral and national development is now more widely appreciated. Reliable, cost-efficient, rural telecommunications can enhance levels of output, employment, and foreign exchange earnings (in export sectors) by enabling a higher utilization of resources. The efficiency gains at the enterprise and worker productivity level can be significant and intermediate. Higher long-term growth rates can also be realized and better use made of all infrastructures — roads, power, water, and other basic inputs into the productive process.

Economies can be readily realized in the deployment of skilled personnel and other savings affected in the use of other scarce resources (e.g., imported petroleum and transport capacity), by the use of a basic telecommunications network to coordinate decision-making and the different stages of production, distribution, and exchange. Information flow and business transactions may be speeded up, and better use made of machinery and expensive capital goods. Rural telecommunications can also help reduce costs in all sectors and, in particular, facilitate and improve the supply and delivery of public services, for example, in the fields of health, education, agricultural extension, and veterinary services.

The range of sectors which could benefit rural areas is comprehensive and covers agriculture, forestry and fishing, mining, manufacturing, infrastructure (e.g., power, meteorology, civil aviation, and public works), banking and financial services, transport in all its modes, commerce, tourism, administration, health, education, and others. Potential economic and social benefits would not be restricted to users of the telephone or only those in rural areas. Non-users could also gain from spillover and multiplier effects while urban beneficiaries would be found and the impact on overall development, and a more balanced infrastructure would facilitate improvement to the quality of life.

Conventional investment criteria for rural telecommunications have been based on measures of the direct financial rate of return to the service-supplying entity. A broader approach is needed to assess the indirect economic and social impact of rural telecommunications investment in order to allow for benefits realized beyond the price paid for the use of services. While these gains accrue outside of the telecommunications sector itself, they are nonetheless of vital importance.

The difficulties which might exist in the quantification of indirect economic benefits should not block their existence. It is proposed, therefore, that feasibility evaluations consider their character and scale in any investment decision, and that public authorities (telecommunications entities and Treasury) accord a greater priority for rural telecommunications as a result. The fact that indirect benefits are certainly not negative and are often highly significant, together with the unique role of rural telecommunications as a broadly interconnecting element in infrastructural, productive and social activity, provides sound justification for weighting them in planning evaluations.

TELECOMMUNICATIONS:
PRIORITY NEEDS FOR ECONOMIC DEVELOPMENT

The need for telecommunications services is generally apparent. In developing countries, wherever public telecommunications facilities of adequate quantity and reliability do not exist, there is widespread recourse to communication systems built by individual business or government units for their own use. While specific institutional networks may be necessary in certain cases, widespread fragmentation results in inefficiency in national resource allocation. These independently operated links are not only more costly than public systems, they are also only a partial substitute since they do not properly interface with each other. In addition, they do not provide access to the wider local and national community which would normally be connected to a well-functioning public system.

The choice of telecommunications vs. other basic forms of two-way communication — personal meetings and postal service (or other means of transporting written messages) — depends on the relative cost, speed, convenience, and reliability of each form. Transportation is critical to the speed and cost of personal meetings and also to the postal service. Yet improved transportation, rather than reducing the demand for telecommunications, can create a greater demand due to the widening community of interest resulting from increased mobility. In recent years, with increasing petroleum prices, telecommunications — by which information and ideas can be efficiently conveyed — and by which transport can be coordinated in advance of need is experiencing an increasing comparative advantage over other forms of two-way communication.

At the beginning of 1977, the total number of telephones in the world was estimated at about 398 million. The developing countries of Central and South America, Africa, and Asia—which have 70 percent of the world population and about 20 percent of world GDP have some 29 million telephones, or about 7.3 percent of the total. Outside North America, most telephone networks are owned and operated by governments.

The number of telephones in service is not higher in many developing countries than in some of the more developed. Recent growth rates for the main continental areas are shown in Table 2. These figures are influenced by the high growth rates in countries such as Japan (11.9%), China (22.0%), Republic of Korea (17.9%), Brazil (10.8%), and Mexico (13.5%), which have substantial industries. However, many smaller and less developed countries also have shown substantial rates of growth.

Examples of the world's distribution of telephones are shown in Table 1.

Among the developed countries, the United States, Sweden, Switzerland, Canada, and New Zealand, all have more than fifty telephones per 100 people, while the rest of the developed countries fall within a range of about ten to fifty telephones per 100 people. Developing countries generally have less than five telephones per 100 people. There are also wide variations between the three developing regions of South and Central America, Asia, and Africa, and there are great disparities in telephone densities among countries within each of these regions. Within an industrialized country, the range of variation in telephone density between cities and non-urban areas is relatively small. In less developed countries, however, a large proportion of telephones is usually concentrated in a few cities, with little or no service in large areas of the rest of the country.

Table 1

World Distribution of Telephones

Area	Millions of Telephones	Percentage of World Population	Percentage of Total World Telephones	Telephones Per 100 Population
Developing Countries: Latin America Africa & Asia	29	71.5	7.3	1.1
North Africa	168	6.0	42.4	72.0
Europe	144	19.6	36.2	18.9
Japan	48	2.8	12.2	43.6
Oceania	8	0.5	21.0	38.1

Source: *Telecommunications Journal*, 1979, Vol. 46, p. 567.

THE CHOICE AND OPTION OF TELECOMMUNICATIONS TECHNOLOGY

Because of the acceleration of telecommunications development and the proliferation of information, economists, political leaders, development economists, and the telecommunications planners are all faced with the problem of choosing the right technology.

In spite of these considerations, there is one thing that is in favor of the developing nation having little or no telecommunications: They can avoid the technological shortcomings that exist in the industrial nations' systems. In developed nations, the systems have evolved over the years, and the capital investment was made for equipment that had long life, usually thirty to forty years. A case in point is that of the switching systems — the step-by-step or cross bar. These older switching systems technologically constrain the development of telecommunications. Because of the long life of some of the equipment, it is financially difficult to upgrade some elements of the national system.

The developing nations, particularly those that can afford the capital investment, have this rare opportunity of using the high technology that exists today, and move straightforward into systems that can be used not only for supporting telephone and television, but can be used to provide those services which enhance the development of education and health.

The development of the rural areas depends on a supply of experienced teachers, medical staff, mechanics, farmers, laborers, electricians, and so on, but the training of all these persons is costly. By using the telecommunications network, the needed skills can be transmitted to the rural areas from the urban centers, providing information as needed, and supplemented with periodic visits for face-to-face consultation.

The environment in most of the African countries lends itself to the use of technologies that are most suited not only to the upgrading of the urban cities but to the development of the rural areas. It is important to remember that the choice of telecommunications technology must be the right one, for once installed, its use will be for the next twenty to thirty years. The development planner must also recognize that the use and availability of telecommunications services can enhance the output of the secondary and tertiary sectors of a developing nation's GNP.

These developments are general concepts which may sound quixotic to the developing nations that lack not only the human skills to utilize a telecommunications system, but most important, the capital to make initial investments for development. Relying on imports of both equipment and trained personnel is a costly venture, and many nations cannot afford such ventures.[32] There are numerous recurring problems that constrain the effort of individual developing nations. One of the major problems is forecasting the demand. The second is finding the resources to adjust the telecommunications program to the differences between the actual and forecast patterns of development. Most underdeveloped nations lack the managerial, technical, and financial ability to do this. Forecasting is distorted because of the hidden demand for services, and this creates the problem of developing realistic cost-benefit data.

For the development economist, this is a crucial area because normally the allocation of scarce resources to develop all infrastructures is based on the cost-benefit analysis process. Cost-benefit analysis fails to consider the true benefits of the telecommunications infrastructure because of the lack of understanding of the economic and social impact of telecommunications.

Wellenius states that this "makes it also virtually impossible to justify telecommunications investment objectively in the face of strong competition from other sectors for scarce resources."

Wellenius further points out that underdeveloped nations lack the input-output data which will reflect the amount of telecommunications used by other economic sectors of the economy. Consequently, telecommunications systems are conceived and designed in a void with respect to other economic development programs. For instance, rural development programs refer to such public utilities as water, electricity, and transportation, but not telecommunications. Although it was emphasized from the start that the climate was right for moving into high technology for some African nations, it poses a serious problem for those having little capital. Those countries depending entirely on the developed nations for equipment, which is characterized by a rapidly changing technology, face a two-fold problem.[33]

CHAPTER II

NOTES

1. Anasiudu, R. C. "The benefits and problems of African countries' participation in INTELSAT." Unpublished doctoral Dissertation, University of Illinois at Champaign-Urbana, 1979.

2. Udofia, C. I. "Africa and the international telecommunication." Unpublished doctoral dissertation. Wayne State University, Detroit, Michigan, 1981.

3. Oziri, M. H. "The evolution of telecommunication in Nigeria: A needs anaysis." Doctoral dissertation. University of New York at Buffalo. *Dissertation Abstract International*, *45*, 01.A., 1984.

4. Sy, J. "Capitalistic mode of the telecommunications market in Africa." Unpublished doctoral dissertation, Howard University, Washington, D. C., 1985.

5. Lerner, D. *The Passing of Traditional Society*. New York: The Free Press, 1964.

6. Lerner, D. *The Passing of Traditional Society*. New York: The Free Press, p. 387, 1968.

7. Stover, J. *Information/Technology in the Third World*. Colorado: Westview Press, Inc., 1984.

8. Hoselitz, F. *Sociological Aspects of Economic Growth*. Glencoe, IL: Illinois University Press, 1977.

9. Parsons, T. *The Systems of Modern Societies*. Englewood Cliffs, NJ: Prentice Hall, 1971.

10. Gerbner, G., P. Cross, and H. Melody (eds.). *Communications Technology and Social Policy*. New York: John Wiley & Sons, 1973.

Chapter II Notes Continued:

11. Rao, L. *Getting the Message Across*. Paris: UNESCO Press, 1975.

12. O'Brien, R. (ed.) *Information, Economics, and Power*. Colorado: Westview Press, Inc., 1983.

13. Fisher, G. *American Communication in a Global Society*. New Jersey: Ablex Publishing Corp., 1987.

14. Cassata, M. and M. Asante. *Mass Communications Principles and Practices*. New York: Macmillan Publishing Corporation, 1979.

15. Williams, F. *The Communication Revolution*. Beverly Hills, CA: Sage Publications, 1982.

16. Blackman, R. "A role for telecommunications in the economic development of Africa and Middle East." Unpublished paper at the University of Colorado, Boulder, 1977.

17. International Telecommunications Union. *Pan-African Telecommunications Network*. Geneva, Switzerland: ITU, 1983, 1986, 1987.

18. Dymond, A. (1987). Reducing the number of missing links. *Telecommunications Policy, 11* (2), 122-132.

19. Pierce, W. and N. Jequier. *Telecommunications for Development*. Paris: Organization for Economic Cooperation and Development (OECD), 1977.

20. World Bank. *Telecommunication Sector Working Paper*. Washington, D. C.: World Bank, 1971.

21. Dickenson, C. "Telecommunications in the developing countries: The relation to the economy and the society." In Polishuk and O'Bryant, *Telecommunications and Development*. Paper presented at the First International Telecommunication Exposition, Atlanta, GA, 1977.

Chapter II Notes Continued:

22. Wellenius, B. "The Role of Telecommunications Services in Developing Countries." Chile: University of Chile, Department of Electrical Engineering. No. 9-GLO-001-11-02, (June 1978).

23. Cherry, C. "The Telephone System: Creator of Mobility and Social Change in Pool." (Telecommunications and Economic Development). Paper presented at the First International Telecommunication Exposition, Atlanta, GA, 1977.

24. Parker, E. "Planning Communication Technologies and Institutions for Development." Paper for East-West Center Conference on Communication Policy and Planning for Development, Honolulu, 1976.

25. International Institute of Communications. (1978). *Issues in Communications*. London: Int. Inst. of Communications (2), 1978.

26. Hudson, H. "Telecommunications and Development in the Canadian North". In Polishuk and O'Bryant, *Telecommunications and Economic Development*. Paper presented at the International Telecommunications Exposition, Atlanta, GA, 1977.

27. Yusuf, R. *World Telecommunication Forum,* ITU, Geneva, (October 1986).

28. Academy for Educational Development*International Issues in Communications Technology and Policy*, Washington, D. C.: AED 1983.

29. United Nations General Assembly Resolution 36/40. Geneva, Switzerland, (November 1984) p. 10.

30. International Telecommunication Union. Pan-African Telecommunications Network Publication, Geneva: ITU, (1972, 1981, 1983, 1987).

31. Lewis, W. *Development Planning*. New York: Harper and Row Publishers, 1966.

Chapter II Notes Continued:

32. Wellenius, B. "Some recurrent problem of telecommunications in developing countries." *IEEE Transactions in Communications*, (7), 723-728, (July 1976).

Additional References:

*   Academy for Educational Development. *International Issues in Communications Technology and Policy*. Washington, D. C.: Academy for Educational Development, 1983.

*   Guttman, W. L. "Telecommunication and sub-Saharan Africa." *Telecommunications Journal, 10* (4), 325, 1986.

*   International Telecommunications Union. *Appropriate Modern Telecommunications Technology for Integrated Rural Development in Africa*. Geneva: ITU, 1981.

*   Miller, B. "The role of ITU in African telecommunications." *African Journal*, 12, 8-9, 1978.

*   Rogers, E. and S. Lyne. *Modernization Among Peasants: The Impact on Communication*. New York: Holt, Rinehart and Winston, 1969.

*   Saunders, R. and J. Warford. "Evaluation of Telephone Projects in Less Developed Countries." *Telecommunication Journal*, Vol. 46, 559-567, 1979.

*   World Bank. *Demographic: World Development Report*. Washington, D. C.: World Bank, 1986.

CHAPTER III
Pan-African
Telecommunications Network
Technological Infrastructure

This chapter will review and analyze the evidence bearing on the development of the PANAFTEL network in the context of its historical background, its present situation, and its potential contribution to development objectives. Telecommunications as they exist in Africa are, at best, limited and inadequate because, in most places, they are only developing at a slow pace. The tendency, almost throughout the continent, is the widening of the gap between rural and other telecommunications services. Unless immediate action is taken, these circumstances could continue to leave the majority of the African population without even the most basic telecommunications services.

Since achieving political independence, the new states have applied themselves to the task of developing their national telecommunications systems. They have also applied themselves to developing their international communication, especially its inter-African dimension. This has not been an easy task due to the almost complete absence of skilled manpower as well as financial and other natural resources in most of the continent of Africa. Nevertheless, African governments have individually and collectively, through organizations such as the Organization of African Unity and the Economic Commission for Africa, decided that a reliable telecommunications infrastructure within and among African countries is an essential element without which there can be no meaningful economic development.

The PANAFTEL network has made some progress because of the efforts of individual African governments, the funding assistance of the International Telecommunications Union and the United Nations Development Program, and of several other multilateral and bilateral financing institutions. As of 1987, twenty-five years after the first idea of a planned African telecommunications network was conceived, considerable progress could be reported. In summary, the PANAFTEL network, as of 1987, consisted of the following, as shown in Figure 1:

- 40 microwave systems between national centers, with a total length of 35,000 kilometers.
- 38 international automatic telephone exchanges.
- 3 coaxial multichannel submarine cables, with a total route length of 8,000 kms.
- 42 countries with semi- or fully-automatic international telex exchanges.
- 73 satellite communication earth stations operating 40 intra-African circuits.
- 6 domestic satellite communication systems operating 64 earth stations.[1]

Most of these systems have been completed since 1970. In addition, several broadband microwave systems, as well as six satellite communication earth stations, have been under construction. This extensive PANAFTEL network provided the transmission paths between national centers. To enable the network to be used fruitfully for telephone and telex communications, it was necessary to equip each national center with an international telephone and an international telex exchange. Thirty-eight of the fifty African countries are equipped with international automatic telephone exchanges, and others are under construction.

Similarly, forty-two out of fifty of the African countries are equipped with modern electromechanical or digital international telex exchanges permitting full automatic service. Direct multichannel circuits have been established between twenty-three countries on a fully automatic or semiautomatic basis. During the past years, studies were carried out and agreement reached in the two largest subregions on tariffs; and operational arrangements were agreed upon for the fullest utilization of the PANAFTEL network. To give a general idea, however, the number of telephone lines for telephone service has been increasing by 5 to 12 percent in recent years. The volume of tariff for the period of 1987-1991 is expected to increase by 4 to 7 percent. With regard to telex services, the growth rate for main lines is expected to increase at more or less the same rate as for the telephone service.

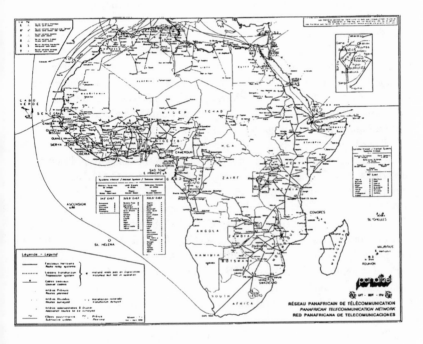

Figure 1. *Pan-African Telecommunications Infrastructure*
as of February 1987 (Map of PANAFTEL).
Source: *Telecommunications Journal*, 1987, Vol. 54, No. XII.

Increases in telecommunications installations on the PANAFTEL network between African states, appear inadequate in comparison with the forecasts made at the Plan Committee For Africa Libreville, in 1983. Expected figures for traffic growth between West Africa, East Africa and Europe and between North America and Africa as a whole for the years 1983-1987 were also high. It is to be recalled that the desire to have a Pan-African telecommunications network was initially formulated at the first meeting of the Regional Plan Committee for Africa in Dakar in 1962. This is, perhaps, the date when PANAFTEL may be said to have been conceived.[2]

Following a fairly long period of difficult and detailed studies conducted in 1986 by the ITU, it was found that approximately 43,000 km of transmission links, of which some 35,000 are microwave and 8,000 submarine cables, were installed. The territorial and submarine systems have been supplemented by satellite communication earth stations operating in forty-one countries. Moreover, forty-three international telephone switching centers and forty-two international telex exchanges were in service in 1986.

These achievements were made possible by the sustained efforts of African telecommunications administrations with the support and assistance of various regional and subregional organizations such as OAU, ECA, African Development Bank (ADB), Pan-African Telecommunications Union (PATU), African Posts and Telecommunication Union (UAPT), Economic Community of West African States (ECOWAS), Southern African Transport and Communications Commission (SATCC), Central African Customs and Economic Union (CACEU), Organization for the Management and Development of the Kagera River Basin (KBO), and the Economic Community of the Great Lakes Countries (CEPGL), as well as such international organizations as the ITU, UNDP, and several multilateral and bilateral financing institutions.

MICROWAVE SYSTEMS OF THE PANAFTEL NETWORK

Until 1987, only analog radio-relay systems were in operation in Africa, although some digital systems were under construction or being planned. In general, the capacity of the systems presently in service is 960 frequency-division multiplex (FDM) circuits. These circuits also provide the capability for the transmission of a color television signal and associated sound channel when required. The frequency bands in use are those standardized by the International Radio Consultation Committee (CCIR) for this transmission capacity, centered on 2, 2, 6, and 6.8 GHz. In some countries the 7 GHz band is also used. The wide variety of equipment being used ranges from equipment of the earlier generation — which has such high power consumption and heat dissipation capacity that it often requires air-conditioning — to the latest, low-consumption, modular equipment — which has reduced maintenance requirements.

REPEATER SPACING OF THE PANAFTEL NETWORK

The spacing between the intermediate frequency (IF) repeaters used by PANAFTEL transmission links is determined principally by the terrain over which the system operates, and to some extent by the climatic conditions over the continent. The spacing can vary from 20 km over flat, tropical areas to over 150 km in mountainous terrain where stations can be sited to provide line-of-sight conditions. The multi-line configurations provide some degree of frequency diversity as a protection against multi-path fading, but in extreme cases this is often complemented by the use of space-diversity antenna.

ANTENNA SYSTEMS OF THE PANAFTEL NETWORK

Near-fed parabolic reflectors are used throughout the PANAFTEL network. These are normally mounted on self-supporting lattice steel towers or stayed masts when modest antenna heights are required. In the event of excessive heights being required, over flat terrain, for example, "periscope" systems consisting of a mast-mounted plane reflector and ground-mounted parabloid antenna are used.

When particularly difficult obstructions are encountered the use of passive repeaters, consisting of one or two large plane reflectors and sited to avoid the obstruction, has proved to be a successful solution. Depending on the frequency, the antenna feeders used are either semi-flexible waveguides or coaxial cables using foam or air-dielectric. In cases of waveguides and air-dielectric cables, pressurizing systems using dry air or inert gas are provided.

POWER SUPPLIES OF THE PANAFTEL NETWORK

Terminal stations, which are located in principal centers, are provided with primary power from the public supply, with a standby motor-generator to maintain the supply in the event of a failure. This primary power is used to flat-charge the batteries that supply the equipment with -24V or -48V D.C. The batteries also provide a degree of autonomy in the event of failure of both the primary supplies.

In the case of isolated repeater stations, a fully autonomous power supply is required because a public source is available only in exceptional cases. This autonomous power is provided by one or more of the following means:

- An arrangement similar to that of the terminal stations, but with the public supply replaced by a motor-generator providing the primary power. The two generators are run in turn for fixed periods, and the battery capacity is usually increased to provide up to twenty hours autonomy;
- A refinement of the above system, using the so-called "charge discharge" technique involving a large battery capacity (of about seventy-two hours autonomy) and a reduction in the running time of the cyclically-operated generators.
- The closed-cycle turbine generator supplied by propane or kerosene burners and operated in a twin-configuration with a battery charger.
- The solar generator, using arrays of solar cells as the primary source to charge a large-capacity battery.

With the advent of low power consumption equipment, the solar generator is now increasingly used as the alternative to the traditional motor-generator arrangement for the autonomous power supplies required for isolated repeater stations through the PANAFTEL network.

<u>OTHER PANAFTEL TRANSMISSION MEDIA</u>

At the present, the analog terrestrial radio-relay system has proved to be an efficient means of providing large numbers of high quality national circuits throughout Africa. At the same time, the convenient interconnection of the circuits for international use has certain limitations presented by distance and terrain which precludes its universal adoption on the continent. For example, it is well known that the quality of transmission, in the case of analog systems, is critically dependent on the length of the circuit and on the number of modulation/demodulation processes and 2-wire/4-wire transformations. In Africa, the length of these terrestrial connections can exceed 6,000 km and involve more than 100 radio-relay sections in tandem— apart from many switching points. Given the often difficult terrain over which these sections are constructed, it is obvious that the grade of service (as well as the transmission quality) can be seriously affected by maintenance problems. Thus, for some, long-distance international media are used. These include the following:

- <u>THE PANAFTEL SUBMARINE CABLE SYSTEMS</u>. For long-distance, point-to-point connections requiring a high circuit capacity, the submarine cable has distinct advantages over other transmission media. Although they obviously have to be used to connect coastal centers, these centers form important international gateways for hinterland countries in the region. A submarine cable is used on the PANAFTEL network to connect Rabat and Lagos, via Dakar and Abidjan, while a further system is being used for the East Coast of Africa.

• THE PANAFTEL EARTH SATELLITE SYSTEM. The obvious advantages of this transmission medium, which is most suitable for long-distance, multi-destination connections of relatively low capacity, are exploited both nationally and internationally on the PANAFTEL network. In this case, the transmission quality is not limited by distance. The system can be used for both short- and long-haul point-to-point routes to establish circuits where it is impractical to install terrestrial links, and also to provide back-up facilities where terrestrial links exist.

In the PANAFTEL context, the vast distances and difficult terrain between the Eastern and Western regions, for example, preclude the use of terrestrial radio-relay systems, and satellite circuits are of necessity included in the routing plans for Africa. The principal disadvantage of satellite circuits — the long propagation time — makes it necessary to recommend the inclusion of not more than one such circuit in any international connection. Adherence to the PANAFTEL routing and switching plans should ensure that this condition is met in most cases.

Forty-one African countries operated at least one earth station within the INTELSAT-PANAFTEL system for international communications as of 1988, and six other countries had earth stations. Six countries rely on domestic satellite systems for some of their major trunk routes. Difficulties are often encountered when setting up international communications using both domestic and international communication satellite circuits in tandem. Fortunately, the majority of international telephone communications originate and terminate in capital cities, where the international gateway exchanges are located in those countries. The PANAFTEL network has, therefore, utilized the most appropriate system or combination of terrestrial microwave systems, satellite systems, and submarine coaxial cables to meet all technical and operational considerations.

By judicial arrangements of circuit routing, it will be possible to set up, automatically or semi-automatically, high quality telephone communications between any two African countries. Such routing plans have been agreed upon on a sub-regional basis and are in the process of being integrated into a single regional routing plan. Bringing the routing plans into full use requires agreement on tariffs and their division among the originating countries, the destination country, and any intermediate countries being transited. General agreement has been reached, on a sub-regional basis, on tariff charges and on a regional tariff structure which will help PANAFTEL meet its inter-African communications objectives.

CHAPTER III

NOTES

1. International Telecommunications Union. *Pan-African Telecom munications Network*. Geneva: ITU, 1983, 1986, and 1987.

2. PANAFTEL Plan Committee. "Development of Telecommunication Network in Africa." *Telecommunications Journal*, 54 (7), 1987, pp. 416-425.

Additional References:

* AT&T Communications Co. *The World Telephone*. New Jersey: AT&T, 1980

* Saunders, R. and J. Warford. "Evaluation of Telephone Projects in Less Developed Countries." *Telecommunications Journal*, Vol. 46, 1979, pp. 567-569.

CHAPTER IV

An Historical Development and Operational Structure of PANAFTEL

In modern times, with the advent of new communication technologies, the African continent has been literally and dramatically transformed, from a collection of isolated countries with less accessibility to each other than to European and other Western nations into a community of shared "voices in the sky."

Man-made microwave receivers, satellite earth stations, and satellites, superseded by the telephone, telex, radio and television, have catapulted Africa from what has been described as an age of "talking drums" into an era of sophisticated telecommunications facilities and services. Spurred by the efforts of various African governments and agencies in concert with financial and technical expertise of specialized agencies, such as the International Telecommunications Union and the Economic Commission for Africa, the African continent has acquired the communications infrastructure to make the launching of the PANAFTEL possible.

The year 1960 had a special significance for the birth of political independence and telecommunications in Africa. It was the year when political independence was achieved by twenty African countries.[1] With independence came the responsibility of operating the national and international telecommunications services. Also in 1960, the ITU Plan Committee for Africa was established.[2]

On achieving independence, African countries inherited many high frequency radio systems installed by their colonial masters. The records of the

1962 Plan Committee indicate the following total number of international systems existing in Africa at the beginning of 1962:

- 35 High Frequency (HF) radio systems (about 80 scheduled circuits) operating between Africa and other countries;
- 15 High Frequency radio systems (about 50 scheduled circuits) operating between African countries;
- 1 Ultra High Frequency (UHF) radio-relay system operating within the East African community (Kenya, Tanzania, and Uganda);
- 13 land cable or open-wire systems each carrying about 100 circuits between African countries.

There were no microwave radio-relay systems, no satellite communication earth stations, and no submarine telephone cables.

In 1967, the Second Session of the Plan Committee was held in Addis Ababa. The important role that could be played by telecommunications in the context of political, economic, and social development began to be appreciated by the ECA and the OAU.

Early in 1968, the Executive Secretary of ECA and the Secretary-General of ITU prepared a draft request for the Administration of the UNDP for funds to finance the PANAFTEL project. The UNDP released the funds for the preliminary phase and appointed ITU as the executive agency for the project. During the period from December 1968 to the end of 1969, a team of experts visited a total of thirty-eight countries and identified thirty-two international PANAFTEL links with a total route length of 14,140 km which needed detailed studies together with international telephone exchanges, in all involving twenty-two countries.

There was very little change by the end of 1970 in the terrestrial network, but the number of high frequency intra-African circuits increased to more than 170. In addition, the first African satellite communication earth stations in Morocco and Kenya were brought into operation in 1969, but none was used at that time for communication to any African countries. The PANAFTEL systems existed at the end of 1970 (Table 2).

The meeting of African telecommunication administrators was convened by ITU in Addis Ababa between November 30 and December 11, 1972, to consider the final draft reports of the consultants. Attention was given by that meeting to the following:

- traffic and circuit requirements, routing and technical considerations, and
- commercial considerations such as viability and financing.

The period from 1971 to 1975 showed some development in the PANAF-TEL network. Two African telecommunications conferences took place during 1975: the Fourth Session of the Plan Committee for Africa, Kinshasa, Zaire, in April, followed by the second conference on African Telecommunications Administration, also in Kinshasa, in December. Both conferences reviewed the progress being made and, in the case of the Plan Committee, prepared circuit forecasts. The Second African Conference made several decisions with the aim of ensuring close coordination in the implementation of the network.

Table 2

PANAFTEL Links, Routes, Circuits, and Earth Stations as of 1970

PANAFTEL Links	Route	System Capacity (Circuits)	
Nairobi - Dar-es-Salaam	Kenya - Tanzania	96 (UHF)	
Nairobi - Dar-es-Salaam	Kenya - Tanzania	36 (UHF)	
Nairobi - Kampala	Kenya - Uganda	96 (UHF)	
Kampala - Nwanza	Uganda - Tanzania	24 (tropo)	
Kukavu - Bujumbura	Zaire - Burundi	12 (VHF)	
Ndola - Lubumbashi	Zambia - Zaire	13 (VHF)	
Lusaka - Ndola	Zambia	960 (SHF)	
Lusaka - Harare	Zambia - Zimbabwe	36 (VHF)	
Blantyre - Harare	Malawi - Zimbabwe	7 (VHF)	
Lagos - Calabar	Nigeria main trunk	960 (SHF)	
Calabar - Buea	Nigeria - Cameroon	12 (VHF)	
Maputo - Kampala	Mozambique	60 (tropo)	
Algiers - Rabat	Algeria - Morocco	72 (cable)	
Algiers - Tunis	Algeria - Tunisia	22 (cable)	
Tunis - Tripoli	Tunisia - Libya	600 (SHF)	
Satellite Earth Stations	Date (Estimate)	Path	
Rabat, Morocco	standard A	1969	Atlantic Ocean Primary
Nairobi, Kenya	standard A	1969	Indian Ocean Primary

Source: *Telecommunications Journal,* 1984, p. 206.

During this period, several microwave and coaxial cable systems, as well as satellite communication earth stations, were brought into service. In addition, several important microwave broad-band radio-relay systems were constructed on national trunk routes. These trunk routes were intended to be part of the PANAFTEL network. Table (2a) provides an account of PANAFTEL links, routes, circuits, and earth stations constructed between 1970 and 1975.

The Third African Telecommunications Conference was held in Monrovia, Liberia, in December 1980 to review the progress being made in the implementation of the network. Common action to be taken in the future was agreed upon, particularly regarding operational, maintenance, and training matters. During the period from 1976 to 1980, considerable progress was made in the implementation of the PANAFTEL network: eighteen microwave routes were completed as well as twenty-four satellite earth stations and one coastal sub-marine cable (see Tables 2b and 2c). As one can see in these two tables, there were only three PANAFTEL links and routes that were not in service out of the whole network by the year 1980.

By 1980, the following regional and subregional institutions and coordinating bodies had been created. All of these bodies are playing active roles in the PANAFTEL network:

- the Pan-African Telecommunications Union (PATU)
- the Economic Community of West African States (ECOWAS) and its Sub-Committee for Telecommunications of the Transport and Communications Committee;
- the PANAFTEL Coordinating Committee for West Africa;
- the PANAFTEL Coordinating Committee for Central Africa;
- the PANAFTEL Committee for East and Southern Africa established as the Technical Committee of the Regional (East and Southern Africa) Annual Conference;
- the PANAFTEL Coordinating Committee for North Africa.

Since 1980, several new microwave radio-relay systems have been brought into operation, including a submarine cable link for NorthEast Africa. There were also forty-eight earth stations in operation in the fifty-member states of Organization of African Unity. Some of this development has been due to subregional groupings such as the Economic Community of West African States, the Southern Africa Transport and Communications, the Liptako-Gourma project (see Table 2d).

Table 2a

PANAFTEL Links, Routes, Circuits, and Earth Stations
Constructed between 1970 and 1975

PANAFTEL Links	Route	System Capacity (Circuits)
Nauakchott - Rosso	Mauritania - Senegal	360 (cable)
Abidjan - Ouagadougou	Cote d'Ivoire-Burkina Faso	960 (SHF)
Libreville - Kribi	Gabon - Cameroon	30 (tropo)
Douala - Malabo	Cameroon - Eq. Guinea	12 (tropo)
Dolissie - Libreville	Congo - Gabon	12 (tropo)
Aswan - Wadi Halfa	Egypt - Sudan	14 (tropo)
Addis-Ababa - Asmara	Ethiopia - Sudan	960 (SHF)
Lilongwe - Blantyre	Malawi - Mozambique	300 (SHF)
Lilongwe - Mzuzu	Malawi - Tanzania	300 (SHF)
Cotonou - Lome	Benin - Togo	960 (SHF)
Porto Novo - Largos	Benin - Nigeria	48 (UHF)
Kigali - Kampala	Rwanda - Uganda	12 (UHF)
Kigali - Kampala	Rwanda - Burundi	12 (UHF)
Nairobi - Kampala	Kenya - Uganda	960 (SHF)
Nairobi - Dar-es-Salaam	Kenya - Tanzania	960 (SHF)
Yaounde - Gamboula	Cameroon - Central Afr. Rep.	960 (SHF)

Zone	Satellite	Standard	Countries
Atlantic Ocean	Primary	A	Angola, Cameroon, Gabon, Cote d'Ivoire, Madagascar, Mozambique, Nigeria, Senegal, Sudan, Zaire, Zambia

Source: *Telecommunications Journal,* 1984, p. 206.

Table 2b

PANAFTEL Links, Routes, Circuits Constructed between 1976 and 1980

PANAFTEL Links	Route	System Capacity (Circuits)
Dakar - Banjul	Senegal - Gambia	300 (SHF)
Dakar - Casablanca	Senegal - Morocco	640 (submar. cable)
Dakar - Abidjan	Senegal - Cote d'Ivoire	480 (submar. cable)
Ziguinchor - Bissau	Senegal - Guinea Biss.	60 (UHF)
Monrovia - Abidjan	Liberia - Cote d'Ivoire	600/120 (SHF/tropo)*
Monrovia - Freetown	Liberia - Sierra Leone	600 (SHF)
Ouagadougou - Lome	Burkina Faso - Togo	960 (SHF)
Lome - Cotonou	Togo - Benin	960 (SHF)
Lagos - Cotonou	Nigeria - Benin	960 (SHF)
Maiduguri - N'Djamena	Nigeria - Chad	960 (SHF)*
Koussari - N'Djamena	Cameroon - Chad	960 (SHF)*
Brazzaville - Impfondo	Congo	960/48 (SHF/tropo)**
Bujumbura - Bukavu	Burundi - Zaire	48 (UHF)
Kinshasa - Brazzaville	Zaire - Congo	120 (SHF)
Lusaka - Chipata	Zambia	960 (SHF)***
Rabat - Algiers	Morocco - Algeria	1260 (coaxial cable)
Tunis - Algiers	Tunisia - Algeria	960 (SHF)
Tripoli - Algiers	Libya - Algeria	960/300 (SHF/cable)

    * Not in service
   ** Route to Central African Republic
 *** Route to Malawi and Mozambique

Source: *Telecommunications Journal*, 1984, p. 207.

Table 2c

INTELSAT Earth Stations Established during 1976-1980

Zone	Path	Standard	Countries
Atlantic Ocean	Primary	A	Algeria, Congo, Egypt, Ethiopia, Kenya, Libya, Nigeria, Togo
	Primary	B	Mali, Sao Tome & Principe
	Major I	A	Cote d'Ivoire
	Major I	B	Gambia, Guinea, Liberia, Mali, Uganda, Burkina Faso
Indian Ocean	Primary	A	Libya
	Primary	B	Burundi, Djibouti, Malawi, Niger, Seychelles, Somalia, Tanzania

Source: *Telecommunications Journal*, 1984, p. 207.

SATELLITE SYSTEMS OF PANAFTEL

The PANAFTEL network is often thought of as a terrestrial system made up of microwave radio systems and coaxial cables. In 1970, only two INTELSAT earth stations were in operation in Africa (Morocco and Kenya). By mid-1983, there were fifty-five INTELSAT international service earth stations in operation in African countries, including the ones under construction (see Tables 2e and 2f).

In the PANAFTEL context, the vast distances and difficult terrain between the Eastern and Western regions precluded the use of terrestrial radio-relay systems, and satellite circuits were of necessity included in the routing plans for Africa. The main disadvantage of satellite circuits is the long propagation time which makes it necessary to recommend the inclusion of not more than one such circuit in any international connection. Adherence to the PANAFTEL routing and switching plans ensure that this condition is met in most cases.

Satellite circuits are integral parts of the regional and subregional routing plans. Satellite circuits are especially important for links between distant countries. They are also of importance between adjacent countries in cases where the terrestrial links are not yet completed. Forty links between African countries are being operated through INTELSAT satellites. In 1983 seven countries were operating sixty-six INTELSAT Standard 2 earth stations for domestic communications; forty-one others were under construction.

The obvious advantage of the satellite systems is that they are most suitable for long-distance, multi-destination connections of relatively low capacity. They also exploit both national and international links of the PANAFTEL network. Satellite transmission quality is not limited by distance as the system can be used for both short- and long-haul point-to-point routes to establish circuits where it is impractical to install terrestrial links and also to provide backup facilities where terrestrial links exist.

OPERATION OF THE PANAFTEL NETWORK

Intra-African routing of telephone communications on an automatic or semi-automatic basis is being provided or planned on a subregional basis with each region being interconnected through traffic concentration centers, each subregion having two or three traffic concentration centers. To facilitate coordination and routing, Africa has been divided into five subregions, two of which (the East and Southern) find it convenient to operate as a combined subregion. These subregions are:

Table 2d

PANAFTEL Links Constructed between 1980 and 1985

PANAFTEL Links	Route	System Capacity (Circuits)
COMPLETED		
Dakar - Bamako	Senegal - Mali	960 (SHF)
Bamako - Bobo Dioulasso	Mali - Burkina Faso	960 (SHF)
Conakry - Freetown	Guinea - Sierra Leone	960 (SHF)
Abidjan - Lagos	Cote d'Ivoire, Nigeria	480 (cable)
Ouagadougou - Niamey	Burkina Faso - Niger	960 (SHF)
Cotonou - Niamey	Benin - Niger	960 (SHF)
Brazzaville - Pointe	Noire - Congo	960 (SHF)*
Kigali - Bukawu	Rwanda - Zaire	SHF/UHF
Assab - Djibouti	Ethiopia - Djibouti	48 (UHF)
Nairobi - Dar-es-Salaam	Kenya - Tanzania	960 (SHF)**
UNDER CONSTRUCTION FOR COMPLETION IN 1985		
Bamako - Conakry	Mali - Guinea	960 (SHF)***
Sikasso - Korhogo	Mali - Cote d'Ivoire	960 (SHF)***
Kedougou - Mali	Senegal - Guinea	960 (SHF)***
Conakry - Abidjan	Guinea - Cote d'Ivoire	960 (SHF)
Conakry - Monrovia	Guinea - Liberia	960 (SHF)
Abidjan - Accra	Cote d'Ivoire - Ghana	960 (SHF)
Accra - Lome	Ghana - Togo	960 (SHF)
Accra - Ouagadougou	Ghana - Burkina Faso	960 (SHF)***
Birni Nkani - Sokoto	Nigeria - Niger	120 (SHF)***
Djibouti - Hargeisha	Djibouti - Somalia	960 (SHF)
Kitale - Sudan Frontier	Kenya	120 (SHF)****
Lusaka - Linlogwe	Zambia - Malawi	960 (SHF)
Livingston - Bulawayo	Zambia - Zimbabwe	960 (SHF)*****
Francistown - Bulawayo	Botswana - Zimbabwe	960 (SHF)*****
Mbabane - Maputo	Swaziland - Mozambique	960 (SHF)
Djibouti - Cairo	Djibouti - Egypt	cable/ unknown******
Fada N'Gourma - Porga	Burkina Faso - Benin	SHF/unknown***
Mopti - Ouagadougou	Mali - Burkina Baso	SHF*******
Gao - Niamey	Mali - Niger	SHF*******
Dori - Tera	Burkina Faso - Niger	UHF*******

* Route to Angola	** Second route	
*** ECOWAS INTELCOM 1	**** Route to Sudan	
***** SATCC	****** Europe - South East Asia Submarine cable	
	******* Liptako - Gourma Project	

Source: *Telecommunications Journal*, 1984, p. 207.

Table 2e

INTELSAT Earth Stations Established between 1981 and 1983

Zone	Path	Standard	Countries
Atlantic Ocean	Primary	B	Cape Verde
	Major I	A	Niger, Nigeria, Uganda
	Major I	B	Angola, Central African Republic
	Major II	A	Malawi
	Major II	B	Lesotho, Swaziland
Indian Ocean	Primary	B	Rwanda

Table 2f

INTELSAT Earth Stations Constructed between 1980 and 1984

Zone	Path	Standard	Countries
Atlantic Ocean		A	Benin, Mauritania, Tunisia, Zimbabwe
Atlantic Ocean	Major I	A	Egypt
	Major II	A	Nigeria

Source: *Telecommunications Journal*, 1984, p. 207.

North Africa: Five countries (Algeria, Egypt, Libya, Morocco, and Tunisia).

West Africa: Sixteen countries (Benin, Cape Verde, Gambia, Ghana, Guinea-Bissau, Cote d'Ivoire, Liberia, Mali, Mauritania, Niger, Nigeria, Senegal, Sierra Leone, Togo and Burkina Faso).

Central Africa: Eleven countries (Angola, Burundi, Cameroon, Central African Republic, Republic of Chad, Congo, Equatorial Guinea, Gabon, Rwanda, Sao Tome and Principe and Zaire).

East and South Africa: Eighteen countries (Botswana, Comoros, Djibouti, Ethiopia, Kenya, Lesotho, Madagascar, Malawi, Mauritius, Mozambique, Seychelles, Somalia, Sudan, Swaziland, Tanzania, Uganda, Zambia and Zimbabwe).

Each subregion has adopted its own telephone routing plan and has agreed to a common tariff policy. The commencement of the operation of the routing plans requires both transmission links and switching centers, with the terrestrial and spatial transmission links, together with the international telephone exchanges.

Table 3 gives an account of PANAFTEL's international telephone exchanges, as of 1983, in fifty African countries, with associated equipment. This configuration allows telephone traffic to European and Western countries, or to another African country, to be originated or terminated in all African countries.

Since achieving political independence, the new African states have applied themselves to the task of developing their national telecommunications systems as well as their international communications links, especially to other African states. This has not been an easy task because of the almost complete absence of skilled staff at all levels, the lack of material and financial resources, and, last but not least, the peculiar topographical and climatical conditions existing in most parts of the continent of Africa. In 1984, Butler described the situation as follows:

"The Pan-African Telecommunications Network, PANAFTEL, has progressed far beyond the stage of constituting the backbone of an African regional network. It is gradually developing into an instrument of communication for connection with other continents. For this reason, it also has undeniably become a stimulating factor in the development of national networks. Indeed, a project such as PANAFTEL can never be completed since it is developing concurrently with social, economic and cultural advances in Africa and takes advantage of the great strides made in technology and telecommunications systems.

Table 3

PANAFTEL International Telephone Exchanges (at the end of 1983)

System	Location
Crossbar (24)	Algeria, Angola, Burundi, Cameroon, Congo, Djibouti, (RFS 1983), Ethiopia, Gabon, Cote d'Ivoire, Kenya, Liberia, Libya, Madagascar, Morocco, Niger, Rwanda, Senegal, Swaziland, Tanzania, Togo, Tunisia, Uganda, Zaire (RFS 1984), Zambia
Electronic and Semi-electronic (14)	Benin, Egypt, Ghana (RFS 1984), Guinea (RFS 1984/85), Lesotho (1984), Malawi, Mali (RFS 1984), Mauritius, Nigeria, Seychelles, Sierra Leone, Sudan, Burkina Faso
N/A	Botswana (RFS 1984), Cape Verde (RFS 1984), Gambia (RFS 1984), Guinea-Bissau (RFS 1984), Mauritania (RFS 1985)
N/A	Central African Republic, Chad, Comoros, Equatorial Guinea, Mozambique, Sao Tome and Principe, Somalia

Source: *Telecommunications Journal,* 1984, p. 209.

A proof of this is resolution No. CM Res. 885 (XXXVII) adopted by the OAU Council of Ministers in 1981, which extended PANAF-TEL activities to the national networks and thus presaged an overall intersubscriber structure making the best possible use of the various technical resources for the transmission, switching and distribution of data signals. The growing extent and complexity of the network and the requirements of adequate service; quality and availability call for increasingly strict standards with regard to plan management, training of personnel, operation and maintenance. It will thus be seen that the task is an enormous one and that financing needs can only be met by adopting completely innovatory solutions.[3]"

Nevertheless, the African governments, individually and collectively through organizations such as the OAU, ECA, and others, have concluded that a good, reliable telecommunications structure within and between African countries could be an essential infrastructure without which there could be no meaningful economic development, thereby stimulating their interest to pursue the full implementation of PANAFTEL development programs.

PANAFTEL-North (North Africa Subregional Network)

Hizekiel Issac delineates the common cause for a regional endeavor:

Today the lack of infrastructure, telecommunications being outstanding, stands out as the major obstacle to intra-African cooperation, and intra-African trade, both essential for the development of our continent.[4]

This endeavor in a Pan-African telecommunication network, is viewed as a great regional venture in telecommunications development. The developmental situation of the countries in the North African subregion favors the total development of bilateral links and relations, as well as direct links with the countries of the Mediterranean Basin and the Arab world as a whole.

Relations to the south of North Africa and with other countries of the continent, however, are still inadequate. Mauritania's networks should be extended towards West Africa; the North African networks and those in Sudan should connect East Africa to Egypt. As things stand, only the submarine cables between Morocco and Senegal, and Djibouti and Egypt enable direct links to be established with the other African subregions. The number of telephone lines in the countries of the subregion has increased at an annual rate of roughly 15 percent, and the telephone density in that part of the continent, which now stands at 2.5 percent, is higher than in the other subregions. The number of telex lines has doubled in the past five years.[5]

All the eight North African Arab state network are part of the Middle East and Mediterranean Telecommunications Network (MEDARATEL) (see Figure 2) superimposing the PANAFTEL. The eight countries are: Algeri Bahrain, Egypt, Libya, Morocco, Mauritania, Sudan, Somalia, and Tunisia.

Even though these countries own a participatory share in the INTELSAT system, they also own shares and receive various telecommunications services from the Arab Satellite Communication System (ARABSAT). Table 4 show PANAFTEL-North, which is part of MEDARABTEL and has membershi shares in ARABSAT. Libya and Egypt dominate the subregion's investment share and total number of circuits. The two nations have a total of 668 circuits out of the 773.

PANAFTEL-West
(Subregional Network of The Economic Community of West African States Telecommunications Network)

Massive infrastructural telecommunications development within the Economic Community of West African states (ECOWAS) subregion with associated problems and constraints is a topic of interest to communication and development experts. A description of development and plans to establish a subregional medium capacity telephone exchange to handle border traffic to integrate member states systems, known as (INTERCOM), is elaborated in this section of the study.

ECOWAS decision-makers have recognized telecommunications develop-ment as a vital tool in the subregion's economic and social progress. There is evidence provided to suggest that ECOWAS may achieve its development goals.[6]

GENERAL OVERVIEW OF ECOWAS

The Treaty of Lagos, which established ECOWAS, was signed in May 1975 by fifteen states, with the objectives of promoting trade, cooperation, and self-reliance in West Africa.

Outstanding protocols bringing certain key features of the treaty into effect were ratified in November 1976. Cape Verde joined in 1977. ECOWAS member states are as follows:

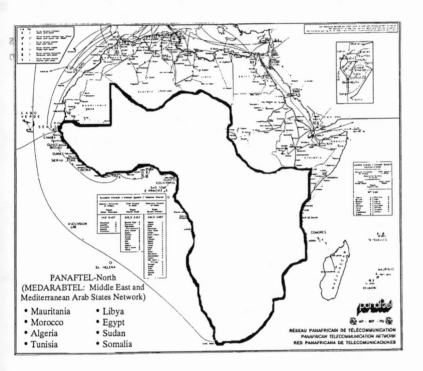

Figure 2. <u>Middle East and Mediterranean Arab States Network</u>
Source: *Telecommunications Journal*, 1987, p. 422

Table 4

List of Shares in Arab Space Communication Organization's
Capital Calculated on a Basic Capital of 100 Million US Dollars

Serial No.	State	Rate of Sharing %	Value in US$	Value of First Payment in (1000)	Total Number of Half-Circuits*
2	Libya	18.2	18.2	925	434
3	Egypt	10.4	10.4	520	234
11	Sudan	2.1	2.1	105	48
13	Algeria	0.9	0.9	45	21
17	Tunisia	0.6	0.6	30	13
18	Morocco	0.5	0.5	25	12
19	Somalia	0.3	0.3	15	6
20	Mauritania	0.2	0.2	10	5
Total		100.0	100.0	5000	773

* Represents the half-circuits occupying two low-power transponders for
the purposes of domestic voice and television based on the equivalent of
200 voice circuits equal one transponder, and for this purpose of calcul-
ations only.

Source: *Telecommunications Journal,* 1977, Vol. 44, No. IX, p. 423.

Benin	Guinea-Bissau	Niger
Burkina Faso	Cote d'Ivoire	Nigeria
Cape Verde	Liberia	Senegal
The Gambia	Mali	Sierra Leone
Ghana	Mauritania	Togo
Guinea		

ECOWAS ORGANIZATION

The head of states and governments meet once a year. The chairman is drawn from different member states, in turn. The Council of Ministers, consisting of two representatives from each country, has a chairman who is drawn from each country, in turn. This council meets twice a year and is responsible for the running of the community. The ECOWAS treaty provides a community tribunal whose composition and competence are determined by the authority of heads of states and governments; it interprets the provisions of the treaty and settles disputes between member states that are referred to it. The headquarters of the executive secretariat is in Lagos, Nigeria. The executive secretary is elected for a four-year term, which may be renewed once only. There are four specialized commissions of ECOWAS: 1) Trade, Customs, Immigration, Monetary and Payments; 2) Industry, Agriculture and Natural Resources; 3) Transport, Communications and Energy; 4) Social and Cultural Affairs.

ACTIVITIES

ECOWAS aims to promote cooperation and development in economic, social, and cultural activity particularly in the fields for which a special commission has been appointed to raise the standard of living of the people of the member countries, to increase and maintain economic stability, to improve relations among member countries, and to contribute to the progress and development of Africa. The treaty provides for compensation for states whose import duties are reduced through trade liberalization and contains a clause permitting safeguard measures in favor of any country affected by economic disturbances through the application of the treaty. The treaty also contains a commitment to abolish all obstacles to the free movement of people, services, and capital, and promote harmonization of agricultural policies, common projects in market research, the agriculturally-based industries, joint development of economic and industrial policies, and elimination of disparities in levels of development and common monetary policies.

ECONOMIC DEVELOPMENT

ECOWAS undertook a critical appraisal of economic conditions in member states in 1979 and 1980 to provide information for development planning. The Nigerian Institute of Social and Economic Research coordinated the survey, and other institutions and universities were called upon to take part. In September 1978, a meeting of Customs and Statistics Experts was convened in Lagos to consider the problem of different standards in the region; this led to the adoption of common customs and statistical nomenclature and a code of standards and definitions. Pre-feasibility studies on the establishment of a private regional investment bank were undertaken by ECOWAS Secretariat in 1984. The creation of the bank (known as Ecobank, based in Lome, Togo) was approved by heads of states and governments in November 1985. ECOWAS has announced the establishment of Ecobank Transnational, Inc. The aims of the bank are to promote intra-ECOWAS trade to support facilities for projects, to provide technical assistance for projects, and to promote investments of private and public resources.

The West African Industrial Forum, sponsored by ECOWAS, is held every two years to promote regional industrial investment. The sixth Forum was held in Dakar, Senegal, in December 1984, with assistance from the European Community and UNIDO. During 1984-85 the Secretariat identified several possible industrial enterprises to be undertaken as part of a regional industrialization scheme.

The world telephone statistics for 1980 reveal that Africa has the lowest telephone density in the world — 1.0 telephone instrument per 100 inhabitants. ECOWAS, as a subregion, has the same density.[7] As part of the findings the study reveals the following:

1. Most ECOWAS member states do not as yet possess even the minimum telecommunications facilities necessary for government to exercise satisfactorily the basic functions in matters of administration in all parts of the state.
2. In many cases, telecommunications traffic between ECOWAS member states had to be routed through fairly remote non-ECOWAS states, even in cases where the ECOWAS member states share a common border.
3. Available international telecommunications traffic links were inadequate both in quantity and performance standards.

4. Because of the geography and demography of the subregion,
   a good telecommunications link could act as a life to a community,
   making its existence highly precious.

The world telephone statistics, as of January 1977, indicated that the telephone density on the entire African continent was only 0.4 per 100 people. This figure implies that many telecommunications administrations have not been able to meet demand and are providing less than adequate service, resulting in telecommunications not being permitted to play their role in contributing to overall economic growth *(Telecommunications Journal,* 1980). The telephone penetration in ECOWAS member states is shown in Table 5. By assessing the figures, one can say that almost all the member states need to increase their DEL telephone apparatus with respect to their population.

Corresponding statistics for broadening (Table 6) indicate penetration of broadcasting in the ECOWAS member states. As the record shows, some of the member states only have one radio and television station, and there is no doubt that a nationwide breakdown in communication cannot occur. Through the assessment of facilities, it is evident that there is a need for more radio and television stations with subsequent receiver sets to support the overall fundamental goal of PANAFTEL infrastructure.

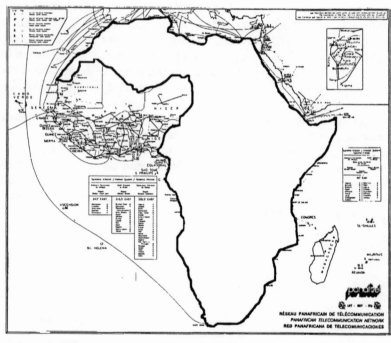

PANAFTEL - WEST
(ECOWAS Subregional Network)

- Mauritania
- Senegal
- Gambia
- Guinea-Bissau

- Guinea
- Mali
- Sierra Leone
- Liberia

- Cote d'Ivoire
- Cape Verde
- Burkina Faso
- Benin

- Ghana
- Togo
- Nigeria
- Niger

Figure 3. PANAFTEL-WEST Linking ECOWAS Member States
Source: *African Telecommunications Report*, December 1987, p. 7.

Table 5

Telephone Penetration in ECOWAS Member States

Country	Population (x100)	Direct Exchange Lines (DEL)	Telephone Apparatus	DEL/100inh Apparatus/ 100inh	
Benin	3197	5400	1033	0.17	(0.32)
Burkina Faso	5938	4000	8600	0.07	(0.14)
Cape Verde	273	1490	1570	0.55	(0.58)
Cote d'Ivoire	7188	27600	66600	0.38	(0.93)
Gambia	494	1470	2500	0.30	(0.51)
Ghana	10000	36100	64900	0.36	(0.65)
Guinea	5143	6600	9500	0.13	(0.18)
Guinea-Bissau	791	N/A	2200	N/A	(0.28)
Liberia	1500	N/A	7500	N/A	(0.50)
Mali	5697	3300	5700	0.06	(0.10)
Mauritania	1318	2677	N/A	0.20	(N/A)
Niger	5246	5200	7800	0.10	(0.15)
Nigeria	80000	58700	16730	0.07	(0.21)
Senegal	4436	15200	38700	0.34	(0.87)
Sierra Leone	3330	7000	10500	0.21	(0.32)
Togo	2371	5600	10400	0.24	(0.44)

Source: *Telecommunications Journal*, 1980, Vol., No. 47 XII, p. 189.

Table 6

Penetration of Broadcasting in ECOWAS Member States

Country	Radio Stations	Radio Receivers	TV Stations	TV Sets
Benin	1	N/A	1	N/A
Burkina Faso	1	N/A	1	N/A
Cape Verde	2	N/A	N/A	N/A
Cote d'Ivoire	6	206,000	11	154,000
Gambia	2	N/A	N/A	N/A
Ghana	23	1.8 Mill	4	35,000
Guinea	1	N/A	N/A	N/A
Guinea-Bissau	1	N/A	N/A	N/A
Liberia	4	260,000	1	10,000
Mali	1	N/A	N/A	N/A
Mauritania	1	N/A	N/A	N/A
Niger	1	N/A	N/A	N/A
Nigeria	7	5.25	9 Mil (77)	45,000 (77)
Senegal	5	295,000	2	2,000
Sierra Leone	2	315,000	1	15,000
Togo	1	N/A	N/A	N/A

Source: *World Press Encyclopedia,* 1986, Facts on File, N.Y., p. 361.

ECOWAS Telecommunications Growth

Almost half of the population of the ECOWAS subregion lives without electricity which makes communication of any type difficult, not to mention television and telephone.[8] Radio is the best medium of communication in all African countries, and an inexpensive radio gives the rural population the opportunity to hear their national voice and news from abroad. The limited communication facilities in the rural areas create a cut-off from the source of communication flow among villagers.

It seems a foregone conclusion that the whole region needs more and better communication technologies of all types. Oziri's (1984) dissertation gave some highlights on how telecommunications' growth touches many bases in the national development plans, including, responsibility for illiteracy, education, commerce and industry, transportation, trade and banking and, of course, health. ECOWAS's policymakers are aware that telecommunications and information are the most rapidly advancing sectors of every economy. Since the establishment of the community, telecommunications growth has been slow but promising. Until the member state governments allow the private sectors to control their own investments and development, the growth will continue to be slow.

Another setback for ECOWAS telecommunications growth is how to secure venture capital from member states' governments. It remains a serious challenge for ECOWAS member countries to build a reliable telecommunications system. Many international lending institutions have accepted telecommunications as an essential growth factor. Their contributions towards building ECOWAS telecommunications have been increasing in recent years, according to the World Bank.[9] For rapid growth, ECOWAS also needs to examine the availability of non-institutional sources of capital for its telecommunications development. This endeavor will necessitate some new economic and political principles and strategies.

The African states have learned from experience acquired from the implementation of PANAFTEL and the general situation and international telecommunications network in the African region. As a result, the African Development Bank has decided on various courses of action with a view to achieving growth and service quantity objectives by undertaking more sound feasibility studies, for expanding the domestic networks, interstate links, and rural telecommunications, maintaining the existing installations, and improving the financial management of the network. OAU President Nyerere of Tanzania once said: "Growth must come out of our roots, not through the grafting on to those roots of something which is alien to our society. We shall draw sustenance from universal human ideas and from the practical experience of other people; but we start from a full acceptance of our Africaness and a belief that in our own past there is much which is useful for our future."[10] The Secretariat of ECOWAS has been doing more studies on the telecommunications network in West Africa in order to pinpoint the areas which require immediate attention. Member countries are independently channeling large portions of their development funds toward the improvement of links with their neighbors among the new cable system between Nigeria and Cote d'Ivoire. This link will serve a critical function within ECOWAS, connecting the two most economically active countries in the sub-region.

THE ECOWAS SUBREGIONAL NETWORK

The concept of flow signifies the movement of communications in their widest sense—messages and images, ideas and entertainment, technology and capital, personnel and ideologies within and between societies. The ECOWAS subregional telecommunications infrastructure is a unique one. The multi-language system, different lifestyles, culture, beliefs, and geographic conditions slows down progress. With all the challenges mentioned above, the subregional telecommunications growth is slow but promising.

ECOWAS' subregion has adopted its own telephone routing plan and has agreed to a common tariff policy. The network comprises both transmission links to each member state and to switching centers, together with an international telephone exchange. Table 9 shows the ECOWAS subregional links, routes, and circuits. It is true that for a telecommunications system to serve a subregion like ECOWAS effectively, it must have certain characteristics:

1. The system must be inexpensive.

2. It must also be reliable and relatively rugged an require no highly sophisticated maintenance and operating personnel.

3. The system should be well-designed to withstand the heat from the Sahara desert and other tropical climates.

4. It should be designed to suit the environment, social, and cultural context.

Table 7

ECOWAS Subregional Links, Routes, and Circuits

Links	Route	System Capacity (Circuits)
Dakar-Bamako	Senegal-Mali	960 (SHF)
Bamako-Bobo	Dioulasso-Mali-Burkina Faso	960 (SHF)
Conakry-Freetown	Guinea-Sierra Leone	960 (SHF)
Abidjan-Lagos	Cote d'Ivoire-Nigeria	480 (Cable)
Ouagadougou-Niamey	Burkina Faso-Niger	960 (SHF)
Cotonou-Niamey	Benin-Niger	960 (SHF)
Bamako-Conakry	Mali-Guinea	960 (SHF)
Sikasso-Morhogo	Mali-Cote d'Ivoire	960 (SHF)
Kedougou-Mali	Senegal-Guinea	960 (SHF)
Conakry-Abidjan	Guinea-Cote d'Ivoire	960 (SHF)
Conakry-Monrovia	Guinea-Liberia	960 (SHF)
Abidjan-Accra	Cote d'Ivoire-Ghana	960 (SHF)
Accra-Lome'	Ghana-Togo	960 (SHF)
Accra-Ouagadougou	Ghana-Burkina Faso	960 (SHF)
Birni Nkani-Sokoto	Nigeria-Niger	120 (SHF)
Fada N'Gourma-Porga	Burkina Faso-Benin	960 (SHF)
Mopti-Ouagadougou	Mali-Burkina Faso	(SHF)
Gao-Niamey	Mali-Niger	(SHF)

Table 7 (continued)

Links	Route	System Capacity (Circuits)
Dori-Tera	Upper Volta-Niger	UHF
Lagos-Calabar	Nigeria main trunk	960 (SHF)
Nouakchott-Rosso	Mauritania-Senegal	360 (Cable)
Abidjan-Ouagadougou	Cote d'Ivoire-Burkina Faso	960 (SHF)
Dakar-Bamako	Senegal-Mali	960 (SHF)
Cotonou-Lome'	Benin-Togo	960 (SHF)
Porto Novo-Lagos	Benin-Nigeria	48 (UHF)
Dakar-Banjul	Senegal-Gambia	300 (SHF)
Dakar-Casablanca	Senegal-Morocco	640 (Submarine Cable)
Dakar-Abidjan	Senegal-Cote d'Ivoire	480 (Submarine Cable)
Ziguinchor-Bissau	Senegal-Guinea-Bissau	60 (UHF)
Monrovia-Abidjan	Liberia-Cote d'Ivoire	600/120 (SHF/ Tropo)
Monrovia-Freetown	Liberia-Sierra Leone	600 (SHF)
Ouagadougou-Lome'	Burkina Faso	960 (SHF)
Lome'-Cotonou	Togo-Benin	960 (SHF)
Lagos-Cotonou	Nigeria-Benin	960 (SHF)

Source: *International Telecommunications Union,* 1986, p. 206.

The ECOWAS member states' utilization of INTELSAT facilities for domestic, intra-African, and intercontinental telecommunications has revolutionized the patterns of flow of telecommunications messages and resources that most of the ECOWAS states inherited from the colonial era. The decolonizing function of satellites requires that technology be invested with a driving force of its own, irrespective of the political, economic, and social factors that shape its use.

Ouagadougou, Bamako, and Dougorona in West Africa are three of the fifty-five relay station sites in a microwave system. Although not the world's longest, the PANAFTEL-West network has been one of the most challenging telecommunications networks to build, maintain, and operate. This microwave project, PANAFTEL-West, linking Senegal, Mali, Burkina Faso (formerly Upper Volta), Niger, and Benin, is part of a master plan conceived by the International Telecommunications Union in 1973 to serve all of Africa with a vast microwave system (see Figure 3).

Some parts of the continent are relatively well-served. However, in western and central Africa, only isolated microwave systems are in operation. The PANAFTEL-West plan calls for linking four sections, totaling some 650 km, to create a 3,000- km path linking Dakar, in Senegal, to Cotonou, in Benin. The linking of these four sections, roughly the distance between Miami and Montreal, is part of the ECOWAS telecommunications infrastructure.

PANAFTEL-South
(Subregional Network of The Southern Africa Development Coordination Conference Telecommunications Network)

Much has been written on the problems of telecommunications development in sub-Saharan Africa and on the lack of progress achieved to date. The present investigation takes a closer look at what is happening in the nine member countries of the Southern African Development Coordination Conference (SADCC). This subregion is, in many respects, a special case since it has achieved a measure of success in the implementation of joint policy and planning initiatives. This outcome is, to a large extent, the result of the countries having the benefit of a clearly identifiable, objective focus and economic independence from South Africa, especially in the areas of trade.

However, the region also has had severe and diverse constraints common to other areas in Africa including drought, deteriorating terms of trade, and military conflicts in Angola and Mozambique. A severe foreign exchange and skill shortage exists in most countries of the region, hence, joint initiatives are not in themselves a panacea. In particular, rapid telecommunications development has been out of the question. An important distinguishing feature is that the countries of the region have collectively recognized the important role of telecommunications in the achievement of economic goals and have made a reasonably concerted effort at establishing a genuinely *regional* infrastructure. They have, on the average, also given the sector a slightly higher investment priority than many other African countries, as indicated in Table 8.[11]

Because telecommunications has been strongly linked with transportation in what the countries of the region perceive to be their primary economic obstacle—the domination of South Africa over their trade—this study looks at the region's telecommunications development in this joint context. In the area of transportation at least, structural dependency on South African trade routes has occurred fairly recently (since the 1960s) and is, therefore, considered reversible. This is not the case with telecommunications, since the region's international links were, from inception, centered on South Africa or the metropolitan countries. However, patterns can be changed and made to contribute to the overall objective. In fact, some success has been achieved and problems are being encountered at the national level in the development of public telecommunications infrastructures. A continuing role for regional cooperation is identified.

BACKGROUND

SADCC's roots go back to the 1960s when Botswana, Lesotho, Malawi, Tanzania, and Zambia became independent. These realities of national independence without well-developed infrastructures and an increasing reliance on South African trade and transport links, were soon issues which occupied the minds of government. As Mozambique and Angola also gained independence in the 1970s, a stronger regional consciousness developed, with each country seeing the need for collective self-reliance.

However, the economic diversity of the region, and the earlier failure of the East African Community and other supranational grouping had led to the general realization that the creation of a full economic community would be difficult and not necessarily desirable. Two other factors also persuaded leaders against setting up a common market. First, in a free-zone, the tendency would be for investment and production to be attracted to the most developed countries at the expense of those which are poor. Second, the region's lack of foreign exchange in all countries except Botswana and Angola, which have large amounts of hard currency from diamonds and oil respectively, precludes free trade. Industrialization and development, in general, should thus rest on carefully negotiated trade or countertrade

Table 8

Telecommunications Investment

Country	Estimated Average Annual Investment, 1985-87 (US$ million)	Investment as Proportion of GDP (%)
Angola	15.0	0.4
Botswana	15.0	1.5
Lesotho	5.0	0.6
Malawi	11.0	0.7
Mozambique	15.0	0.4
Swaziland	4.0	0.6
Tanzania	12.0	0.3
Zambia	30.0	0.8
Zimbabwe	40.0	0.6
Region	**147.0**	**0.6**

Source: *Telecommunications Policy,* June 1987, p. 122.

agreements. The economic community concept emerged out of a decentralized, non-bureaucratic structure which requires maximum participation of the member states but power to set regional objectives and to select projects through regular meetings of a council of ministers.

Following an exploratory conference attended by the five front line states (Botswana, Angola, Mozambique, Tanzania, and Zambia) and potential co-operating partners, the final launch of SADCC took place in 1980 in Lusaka. This followed conclusion of the agreements leading to Zimbabwe's independence and included participation by the remaining independent states of the region— Lesotho, Malawi, and Swaziland. The Lusaka Declaration set four development objectives:

- the reduction of economic dependence, particularly, but not only, on the Republic of South Africa;
- the foregoing of links to create a genuine and equitable regional integration through telecommunication;
- the mobilization of resources to promote the implementation of national, interstate, and regional policies;
- concerted action to secure international cooperation within the framework of SADCC's strategy for economic liberation.

SADCC's style is to emphasize mutual cooperation in recognition of the region's interdependence and to maintain individual responsibility for plans and projects. Since virtually all states are dependent on foreign donors and investors for their development programs, a central role of SADCC is to coordinate and facilitate foreign participation, much as a broker does between donors, investors, and member country agencies.[12]

From the outset, the twin issues of integrating development and reducing dependence on South Africa have been linked. Whereas the nine countries *together* are *potentially* wealthy, possessing adequate energy resources, abundant land, and virtually all the minerals needed for industrialization, *separately*, they are poor. Their market sizes are small individually, but combined they are sufficient to justify production of a range of consumer and intermediate goods. The primary economic and demographic data are shown in Table 9.

Table 9

Economic and Demographic Summary of SADCC

Country	Population (millions)	Area ('000 km)	Population Density (people/ km)	Urban Population (%)	GDP (US$ '000)	GDP per Capita (US$)
Angola	7.9	1247	6	24	3710	470
Botswana	1.1	600	2	20	1020	930
Lesotho	1.5	30	50	13	850	570
Malawi	7.1	94	76	12	1490	210
Mozambique	13.9	802	17	16	3340	240
Swaziland	0.7	17	41	26	620	890
Tanzania	21.7	945	23	14	4560	210
Zambia	6.8	753	9	48	3940	580
Zimbabwe	8.4	391	21	27	6470	770
Region	**69.1**	**4879**	**14**	**20.5**	**26000**	**380**

Source: Demographic, *Telecommunications Policy,* 1987, p. 128.

Regional fragmentation is illustrated by the trade figures. In 1982, intraregional trade accounted for less than 5 percent of the total imports and exports of the region. Exports to South Africa were only slightly higher at around 7 percent of total exports, but imports were significantly higher at thirty percent of the SADCC total. Six of the nine SADCC countries have South Africa as their main trading partner. Six also depend, at least in part, on South African companies for key mineral exports and, in four of the nine, South African firms dominate retail trade. Increasing trade between SADCC members was thus recognized as an essential if SADCC is to develop regional cooperation and to reduce dependence on South Africa.

TRANSPORT AND COMMUNICATIONS

A number of policies have emerged as important to the region's particular development problems, including agriculture — especially drought control, industry, energy, training, and trade. However, the first priorities were transport and communications since it was recognized that without the establishment of an adequate subregional transport and communications system, other areas of cooperation became impractical. South Africa's dominance was seen to be based on its being the focus of regional transport and communications. At the time of SADCC's inception, Johannesburg had become the transit point for air transport, telephone, and telex traffic between many of the region's capitals and for international links. Half of SADCC's cargo was shipped through South African ports. In the case of Zimbabwe, the most industrialized country of the region, this proportion is much higher and was still over 90 percent in 1986.[13]

Because of the special priority given to this sector, a Southern African Transport and Communications Commission (SATCC) was set up in Maputo for coordination purposes, and it is still the only part of SADCC to have a separate legal and administrative status. SATCC has listed and promoted approximately twenty-eight main projects which have been completed. Around 158, representing a total investment of just over US$300 million, are at various stages of implementation. In view of the region's foreign exchange shortages, virtually all of the foreign exchange portions of the project capital costs (over US$260 million) must be financed externally, the vast majority bilaterally. However, the total program is now almost forty percent financed, and a further ten percent is under negotiation. Of the thirty-seven listed telecommunications projects, ten have been completed, and the total cost of those remaining is almost US$400 million (10 percent of SATCC's total), of which approximately two-thirds is financed or under negotiation.

SATCC works in cooperation with the Southern African Telecommunications Administrations (SATA). Representatives of the nine member administrations meet on a regular basis to discuss national planning and technical issues in order to ensure coordination of those elements of their planning which have regional impact. SATCC coordinates and funds the following activities:

- Satellite earth station connectivity within the subregion.
- International telephone and telex switching centers in the member countries.
- Special application telecommunications in support of subregional transportation and meteorological projects.
- Training and personnel development, including the setting up of joint or cooperative programs and ensuring that each major capital project contains a training element. The PANAFTEL network has been substantially implemented through the support of all of Africa's regional and subregional bodies. SADCC regional PANAFTEL links are mostly 960-channel analog microwave systems, though several of the later links are digital. The overview of the SADCC subregional network is shown in Figure 4.

The development of satellite communications for the region has been addressed by several major earth station projects and by a SATCC study on regional harmonization of satellite communications. Each country in the region currently has at least one earth station, however, at present, almost all stations are used exclusively for international links to non-African countries. Zimbabwe, for example, has a total of over 120 satellite circuits serving twelve destinations; six circuits are dedicated to the United Kingdom and Zimbabwe-Malawi (twelve circuits). All other subregional links currently use the PANAFTEL terrestrial network, and several PANAFTEL projects now under construction will greatly improve regional connectivity. However, several countries — Lesotho, Swaziland, Mozambique, and Angola — would remain isolated or with only limited direct connection to other SADCC countries, and thus depend on South Africa to facilitate connection, without the use of satellites.

SUBREGIONAL SUBSCRIBER DEVELOPMENT

Subregional network statistics and a summary of subscriber growth over the years 1983 to 1986 are provided in Tables 10a and 10b. Whereas this period of three years was too short to define long-term trends, these years cover a period when relatively substantial investments have been made. The longer-

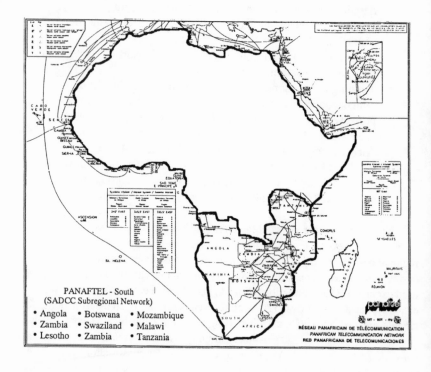

Figure 4. PANAFTEL-SOUTH Showing SADCC Subregional Network
Source: *Telecommunications Journal*, June 1987, p. 125

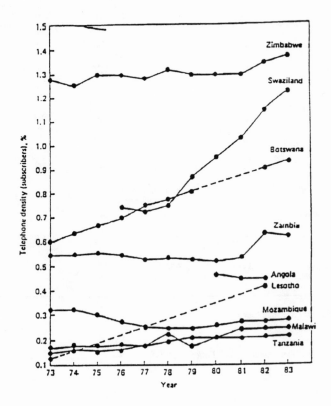

Figure 5. Trend of Telephone Density (1978-1983) of SADCC Countries
Source: *Telecommunications Policy*, June, 1987

Table 10a

SADCC Telecommunications Statistics

Country	DELsa/ in 1986 (thousands)	Telephones in 1986 (thousands)	Registered waiters (thousands)	DELs per 100	DELs annual growth 1983-86 (%)
Angola	46.0	47.0	NAb/	0.6	0.6
Botswana	10.7	21.0	4.36	1.0	4.0
Lesotho	8.9	17.7	5.0	0.6	21.2
Malawi	20.8	44.9	3.8	0.3	6.7
Mozambique	39.1	60.2	28.2	0.3	1.9
Swaziland	8.2	20.0	1.4	1.2	3.5
Tanzania	54.1	116.8	65.5	0.2	7.1
Zambia	47.4	73.4	24.1	0.7	8.2
Zimbabwe	108.2	251.3	35.1	1.3	1.5
Region	**343.4**	**652.3**	**152.8**	**0.8**	**3.9**

a/Direct Exchange Lines
b/No records

Source: *Telecommunications Policy*, June 1987, p. 130.

Table 10b

SADCC Telephone Network Statistics (1986)

Country	Total Exchanges	Automatic Exchanges	Auto Capacity (thousands)	Automatic DELs (thousands)	Percentage Utilization
Angola	59	19	59.9	41.1	69
Botswana	47	19	22.4	10.2	45
Lesotho	43	19	13.2	8.7	66
Malawi	85	31	31.7	19.2	61
Mozambique	145	24	43.9	34.9	79
Swaziland	21	17	14.9	8.1	54
Tanzania	173	35	56.7	42.8	75
Zambia	71	62	75.2	36.1	61
Zimbabwe	97	65	136.2	105.2	77
Region	**741**	**291**	**454.1**	**316.3**	**69**

Source: *Telecommunications Policy*, June 1987, p. 132.

term trend in subscriber density for the ten-year period 1973-83, as indicated in Figure 5, reflects a steady growth for Botswana, Lesotho, and Swaziland, and an almost steady no-growth position in the other countries of the region until the early 1980s. Six SADCC countries still have a telephone subscriber density of less than one exchange line per 100 people. With the exception of Lesotho, current growth rates are below ten percent sometimes considerably less, despite the existence of significant waiting lists of typically twenty to fifty percent of the subscriber base, indicating the presence of a sizable suppressed demand. Evidence from research demonstrates that this kind of telecommunications undersupply represents a considerable economic loss and is likely to be a constraint on growth in the region. Undersupply also means lost revenue to the telecommunications administrations, less than efficient use of the improved regional and international facilities, and reduced internal cash generation and economic independence.

From world comparisons, subscriber density is known to be correlated with a country's per capita income and its level of urbanization. These relationships reflect the level of investment which countries can afford and the cost of bringing new subscribers into the network (rural service is more expensive to provide than urban). A cursory examination of Tables 9 and 10a reveals this trend to be in evidence in the SADCC region; and a broader comparison, using the familiar ITU regression model of per capita GDP and subscriber density, indicates that SADCC countries are not out of line with the world trend. However, the general world model should not be considered normative for low-income countries since, in the current international environment, the value of telecommunications in development is increasingly being recognized and policy emphases are changing. Furthermore, the slow subscriber growth in the subregion over the past few years is explicable through more specific network analysis in most cases. With careful planning, an upturn in the growth rates should be both sustainable and justified. The following factors have been influential:

- Recent emphasis on regional connectivity has, to some extent, concentrated resources into international and main transit switching and to transmission network, to the detriment of subscriber networks. This was perhaps justified in order to lay the basis for future growth and regional connectivity.

- Much of the local network investment carried out over the past five years has involved replacement of obsolete exchange equipment. The emphasis has been on conversion from manual to automatic service.

As noted above, expansion of the subscriber base is required to increase revenues and to improve utilization of the investments already made in national and subregional transmission systems. Expansion into rural areas is also required in order to increase the contribution of telecommunications to national development. In adjusting their emphasis in this way, telecommunications administrations will need to focus more on issues such as local network provision, training, and outside plant maintenance. Attention can still be given to the optimization of regional and international traffic routing, but this attention needs to be based as much on planned subscriber growth as on the rapidly improving regional connectivity facilitated by major transmission projects.

Despite the need for growth, however, the foreign exchange constraints in the region ensure that new investments must be carefully and strategically planned to serve developmental objectives. There are no resources to waste. Highest priority must be given to network expansions which contribute directly to economically productive activities in industry and commerce or to agricultural and rural development programs, including distribution and marketing systems, especially those which generate foreign exchange.

CONCLUSION

Regional cooperation in southern Africa is well-established and has achieved significant gains through the joint planning and promotion of projects which have an impact on the economy and structure of the southern African region. It has also been demonstrated that, at the national level, subscriber development in the public telecommunications networks has been slow and is still at an early stage. Increased attention needs to be given by governments and telecommunications administrations to investment in local networks, to local training and personnel development, to improvement of maintenance, and to other administrative and institutional issues. However, despite this national focus, regional cooperation will continue to be an important factor because of the following contributions it can make:

- coordination and promotion of unfinished rehabilitation and development of the regional network, particularly in Angola and Mozambique;

- continued regional synergy through the coordination of network development and joint promotion of projects for funding, such as satellite sytems, tariffing, and the local repair and manufacture of telecommunications equipment.

Since the particular brand of regional cooperation practiced by the southern African countries is based on strong focal objectives and individual responsibilities rather than bureaucracy, there is good reason to believe that regional planning will continue to be productive and that significant progress will be made in all areas of mutual concern.

PANAFTEL and the International Telecommunications Satellite Organization

The International Telecommunications Satellite Organization (INTELSAT) is an international organization formed in Washington, D.C. in July 1964 to provide international public telecommunications by satellite.[14] Despite the fact that African nations were not invited to the first international conference, by 1967 Algeria, Ethiopia, Libya, Morocco, Nigeria, South Africa, Sudan, Tunisia, and the United Arab Republic (UAR) had joined the consortium and have contributed more than $1.1 million of the $45 million used to establish the system.[15]

Sources of supply for microwave radio systems and associated equipment are manufacturers in Africa. INTELSAT Standard A and B earth stations have been mainly supplied by Japan and France; other sources have been the United States of America and Italy. On the other hand, INTELSAT Standard "Z" earth station equipment for domestic satellite systems has been produced mainly by the United States of America and France.

African nations participating in INTELSAT uplink and downlink their international traffic via INTELSAT's Atlantic Ocean Region and Indian Ocean Region satellites through over sixty INTELSAT Standard A and B earth stations located throughout the continent (see Table 11). Today, African member countries' signatories have over two million investment shares in the INTELSAT global network.[16]

Economically, INTELSAT is a cooperative of owners and users, but it was somehow resolved that the United States investment quota could be 61 percent, although many nations felt that the interim or initial INTELSAT treaties were one-sided in favor of the U. S.[17] Table 12 shows INTELSAT's thirty-six participating African member countries with their signatories and investment shares as of April 1990.

Table 11

African Standards A and B Earth Stations in the Atlantic
and Indian Ocean Regions as of June 1988.

Country	Earth Station Standard	INTELSAT Satellite	Name of Earth Station
Algeria	AAB	(Indian Ocean)	Lakhdaria 3
Angola	-	(Atlantic Ocean)	Cacuaco
Botswana	A	(Indian Ocean)	Kgale
Burkina Faso	A	(Atlantic Ocean)	Songande
Burundi	-	(Indian Ocean)	-
Cameroon	AB	(Atlantic Ocean)	Zamengoe 2
Central African Rep.	A	(Atlantic Ocean)	Mpoko
Chad	-	(Atlantic Ocean)	Goudi
Congo	A	(Atlantic Ocean)	Mouganni
Egypt	AB	(Atlantic Ocean) (Indian Ocean)	Maadi 2
Ethiopia	AB	(Atlantic Ocean) (Indian Ocean)	Sululta 2
Guinea Bissau	A	(Atlantic Ocean)	Bissau
Gabon	A	(Atlantic Ocean) (Indian Ocean)	N'Koltang

Table 11 (continued)

Country	Earth Station Standard	INTELSAT Satellite	Name of Earth Station
Gambia	B	(Atlantic Ocean) (Indian Ocean)	Banjut Banjut
Ghana	A	(Atlantic Ocean)	Nkutunse
Guinea	B	(Atlantic Ocean)	Wonkifond
Cote d'Ivoire	A	(Atlantic Ocean)	Abidjan 1
Kenya	AAB	(Indian Ocean) (Indian Ocean)	Longonot 3
Liberia	B	(Atlantic Ocean)	Sinkor
Lesotho	-	(Atlantic Ocean)	Ha Sofonia
Libya	AB	(Atlantic Ocean) (Indian Ocean)	Tripoli 2
Madagascar	A	(Indian Ocean)	Amoco Madagascar
Malawi	AB	(Indian Ocean)	Kanjedza 2
Mali	B	(Indian Ocean)	Sullymanbougou
Morocco	A	(Atlantic Ocean)	Sehouls
Mozambique	A	(Atlantic Ocean)	Boane
Mauritania	A	(Indian Ocean) (Atlantic Ocean)	Toujounine
Nigeria	AB	(Indian Ocean) (Atlantic Ocean)	Lanlate 2

Table 11 (continued)

Country	Earth Station Standard	INTELSAT Satellite	Name of Earth Station
Niger	AB	(Indian Ocean) (Atlantic Ocean)	Karma 2
Senegal	A	(Atlantic Ocean)	Gandoul
Rwanda	-	(Indian Ocean)	Kicukiro
Sierra Leone	B	(Atlantic Ocean)	Wilberforce
Somalia	-	(Indian Ocean)	Kicukiro
South Africa	AAB	(Indian Ocean) (Atlantic Ocean)	Pretoria 3
Sudan	A	(Atlantic Ocean)	Umm Haraz
Tanzania	-	(Indian Ocean)	Mwenge
Togo	A	(Atlantic Ocean)	Cacavelli
Tunisia	A	(Atlantic Ocean)	Dkhila
Uganda	-	(Indian Ocean)	Kampala
Zambia	AB	(Indian Ocean)	Mwembeshi 2
Zaire	A	(Atlantic Ocean)	N'sele

Key:
A = Atlantic Ocean Earth Station
B = Indian Ocean Earth Station

Source: *COMSAT Publication*, International Earth Stations
(Washington, D.C., 1988), p. 3.

Table 12

INTELSAT African Member Countries, Signatories, and Investment Shares

Country	Signatory	Investment Share
Algeria	Government of the Democratic and Popular Republic of Algeria	0.031398
Angola	Empresa Public de Telecomicacoes (EPTEL)	0.127391
Benin	Office des Postes et Telecoms de la Republique de Benin	0.050000
Burkina Faso	Office des Postes et Telecoms du Burkina Faso	0.068010
Cameroon	Government of the United Republic of Cameroon	0.345284
Central African Republic	Government of the Central African Republic	0.050000
Chad	Societe des Telecommunications Internationales du Tchad (T. I. T.)	0.050000
Congo	Government of the Peoples Republic of Congo	0.050000
Cote d'Ivoire	Government of the Republic of Cote d'Ivoire	0.200366
Egypt	Government of the Arab Republic of Egypt	0.649338
Ethiopia	Telecommunications Service, Provisional Military Government of Socialist Ethiopia	0.129015
Gabon	Societe des Telecommunications Internationales Gabonaises (T. I. G.)	0.050000

Table 12 (continued)

Country	Signatory	Investment Share
Ghana	Ministry of Transport and Communications	0.089954
Guinea	Secretariat d'Etat aux Postes et Telecomms	0.059877
Kenya	Kenya External Telecommunications Company Limited	0.328774
Libya	Government of the Libyan Arab Republic	0.148688
Madagascar	Societe des Telecommunications Internationales	0.0500
Malawi	The Dept. of Post & Telecoms of the Gov't of the Rep. of Malawi	0.112693
Mali	Telecommunications Internationales du Mali (T. I. M.)	0.0103231
Mauritania	Government of the Islamic Republic of Mauritania	0.050000
Mauritius	Overseas Telecomms Services Co. Ltd. of Mauritius	0.190338
Morocco	Government of Morocco	0.179084
Mozambique	Empresa Nacional de Telecomms de Mozambique	0.062527
Niger	Gov't of the People of Niger	0.050000
Nigeria	Nigerian External Telecommunications Limited	0.894590
Senegal	Government of the Republic of Senegal	0.109776

Table 12 (continued)

Country	Signatory	Investment Share
Somalia	Ministry of Post & Telecomms of the Somalia Democ. Republic	0.050000
South Africa	Telkom SA Ltd.	1.144476
Sudan	Government of the Democratic Republic of the Sudan	0.119662
Swaziland	Posts and Telecommunications Corporation (Public)	1.091446
Tanzania	Tanzania Posts and Telecommunications Corporation	0.064473
Togo	Societe Autonome Telecommunications Internationales du Togo (SATELIT)	0.149696
Tunisia	Administration for Post, Telegraph and Telephone of Tunisia	0.050000
Uganda	Ministry of Transport, Communications and Power of the Government of the Republic of Uganda	0.064038
Zaire	Office National des Postes et Telecommunications du Zaire (O. N. P. T. Z.)	0.153676
Zambia	Government of the Republic of Zambia	0.118595
Zimbabwe	Government of Zimbabwe	0.050000

Source: INTELSAT, *Annual Report 1991-92* (Washington, D.C.:
International Telecommunications Satellite Organization), pp. 32-36.

INTELSAT has a decisive role to play in working out solutions to the gamut of telecommunications problems faced by developing nations. The system now provides international public telecommunications services to some 170 political entities and similar domestic services to twenty-four countries. Besides expansion of these systems, maritime mobile service is expected soon. At the same time, advances in technology and economies of scale have enabled INTELSAT to steadily reduce usage charges. Flexibility in leasing arrangements, choice of modulation techniques, earth station size, and transmission plans further enable developing countries to participate in this technology.

INTELSAT has become the world's greatest telecommunications resource, offering a wide range of services to almost 170 countries, territories, and areas of special sovereignty, with additional services planned to meet future needs (see Figure 6). More than fifteen satellites are integrated into the INTELSAT Global Satellite network.[18]

Since the voting power in INTELSAT is still based on the capital investment in the consortium, and also because of the exclusion of African nations in the allocation of INTELSAT contracts, the Third World countries are uncertain of their principal roles in the corporation. By international agreement, INTELSAT must price all services equally, regardless of volume, whether for one telephone circuit or for a thousand circuits. INTELSAT is a nonprofit organization charged with providing service reliably and efficiently to all users. Thus, INTELSAT cannot cost-effectively offer services if high-volume traffic (the cream of the market) is skimmed away; in such an environment, the developing countries with thinner streams of traffic stand to lose the most.[19]

To serve both developed and developing nations, INTELSAT has new telecommunications applications: the global "telelibrary" to make research and technical information available via computer terminals; "telehealth" information systems; and networks for linking specialized research groups together on a regional basis in such areas as agriculture and energy. Taking an even longer term view, INTELSAT has given serious consideration to technologies that may become operational in the 1990s, such as telecommunications-oriented space platforms that could combine a large number of services — space broadcasting, fixed point-to-point telecommunications services, remote data collection, and, possibly, earth resources services — providing new economies of scale of all users.

International telecommunications, while inadequate, is often slightly better in Africa than domestic telecommunications. This stems in many

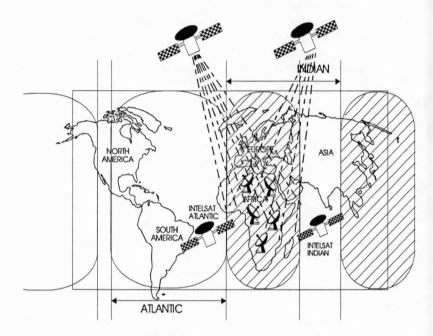

Figure 6. *Concept of INTELSAT System Coverage.*
Source: UNESCO PUBLICATION, *New Communication Order*, 10, 1983, p. 10.

instances from the higher staff salaries which allow the recruitment of more qualified and/or highly motivated personnel. Furthermore, the revenue disparity on international calls permits a higher level of investment and maintenance for the overseas unit. Nevertheless, this additional investment is no guarantee that the demand for long-distance circuits or transponder capacity can be met.

International services are delivered by two methods: satellites and terrestrial (usually microwave) links. Generally, satellite service works admirably and provides the sector with badly needed profits. There are, however, still some problems. First, a majority of African countries (twenty-seven of forty-two countries) use only the INTELSAT Atlantic Ocean satellites. Only seven countries have access to both types of satellite. For the countries without access to both, a multiple hop is required for calls to a significant number of countries in the region and around the world. This reduces transmission quality and ease of connection and, at the same time, drives up access charges.

A second problem is the un-economic use of satellite earth stations. Sub-Saharan Africa has a total of 174 stations, or an average of four per country (one for every two million people). By comparison, Sweden, Denmark, Finland, and Norway—with more than 22 million people—bear a far higher traffic level with just one shared station. Perhaps similar options are not open to Africa because of security concerns or a generalized lack of cooperation in the region. Nevertheless, this plethora of stations entails the expenditure of hundreds of thousands of dollars for each year's additional management and upkeep, when a maximum of one station per country would be more than sufficient.

There is, of course, a link between the inordinate number of satellite receivers and the dreadful problems of the terrestrial long-distance network. For more than twenty years, the ITU and others have been trying to build up the African intercountry links, with only meager success. There are almost thirty sub-Saharan countries without direct communications across at least one of their borders. This results in connections between neighboring countries, such as Sudan and Ethiopia, passing through London and Rome, between Gabon and Congo through Paris, and between Uganda and Burundi through Brussels and Nairobi. Too often even existing links are disregarded and calls continue to pass through European capitals because tariff and exchange arrangements between the users have been ignored or because pressure has been brought against their use by European administrations not eager to lose the access revenues. Some progress has been made by the ITU in planning and surveying additional lines, but the funds needed to complete a comprehensive network and the desire to dispense with the anachronism of trans-hemispheric call connections have not been forthcoming.

CHAPTER IV

NOTES

1. United Nations. *United Nations Yearbook.* Geneva, Switzerland: United Nations   Press, 1961.

2. Tedros, G. "The development of the Pan-African Telecommunication Network (1960-1983)." *Telecommunications Journal*, 51 (4), 1984, pp. 204-210.

3. Butler, R. *Pan-African Telecommunications Network.* Geneva, Switzerland: International Communication Union, 1984.

4. Secretary-General of the Organization of African Unity's Speech, Adiss Ababa: OAU, (April 1976)

5. *African Telecommunications Report.* October 1987.

6. "Africa South of the Sahara." *Europa Publication.* London: Europa Publication Ltd., 1985.

7. AT&T Communications Co. *The World Telephone.* New Jersey: AT&T, 1980.

8. UNESCO. *Cultural Development: Some Regional Experience.* Paris: UNESCO Press, 1981.

9. McLenaghan, J. *Currency Convertibility in the ECOWAS.* Washington, D. C.: International Monetary Fund. LC NO. 17131, 1982.

10. *Spectator Newspaper.* President Julus K. Nyerere of Tanzania's OAU Conference Speech, 1984.

Chapter IV Notes Continued:

11. Dymond, A. "Reducing the number of missing links." *Telecommunications Policy,* 11 (2), 1987, pp. 122-132.

12. EIU Special Report. *SADCC: Progress Projects and Prospects: The Trade and Investment Future of the Southern African Development Coordination Conference.* London, No. 182, 1984.

13. Staff. "Financing Pan-African telecommunication project." *Financial Gazette.* Harare, Zimbabwe, (October 1986).

14. Snow, M. "INTELSAT: An international example." *Journal of Communication,* 30, 1984, pp. 400-412 .

15. Moulton, E. J. "Satellite over Africa." *African Report,* (May 1967) pp. 15-18.

16. International Telecommunications Satellite Organization (INTELSAT). *Annual Report.* Washington, D. C.: INTELSAT, 1991-1992.

17. U.S. Department of State. *Agreement Establishing Interim Arrangements for a Global Commercial Communication Satellite* (Publication No. 51, 313). Washington, D. C.: Government Printing Office, 1964.

18. Till, D. *World Communication Year: New Communication Order,* 8, 9, 10, Paris: UNESCO: Communication Documentation Center, 1983.

19. Pelton, J. *World Communications.* New York: Longman, 1984.

Additional references:

* COMSAT Corporation. *International Earth Stations,* Washington, D. C., 1988.

Chapter IV Notes Continued:

* Ezenwa, U. *ECOWAS and the Economic Integration of West Africa.* New York: St. Martin's Press, 1983.

* ITU: International Telecommunications Union. *Pan-African Telecommunications Network.* Geneva, Switzerland: 1983, 1986 and 1987.

* Smith, D. *The ECOWAS: Prospects and US Policy Implication.* Lagos, Nigeria: Economic Commission for West African States (ECOWAS), 1986.

* Southern African Development Coordination Conference (SADCC). *Inter-Regional Trade Study.* Bergen, Norway, DERAP: 1986.

* "The economic community of West African states." *West Africa,* (June 1981) pp. 1207.

* "Organization of African Unity: 22 years after." *Spectator,* (March 1985) p. 12.

* Uka, E. *ECOWAS and the Economic Integration of West Africa.* New York: St. Martin's Press, 1983.

* *World Press Encyclopedia.* New York: Facts on File, 1986.

CHAPTER V

Financing Telecommunications Development In Africa

Reliable evidence shows that there has been serious underinvestment in telecommunications development in Africa. This chapter analyzes the situation and reasons for this shortfall and explores the major restrictive factors, particularly on the development of the Pan-African telecommunications network. The absence of reliable data makes it difficult to estimate the volume of capital required for the whole infrastructure.

African governments have been obliged to adopt programs involving considerable reduction in public spending and restructuring as part of policy adjustments. The burden of debt threatens all sectors of economic and social development in African countries. The insufficiency of external resources and domestic savings compels governments to make difficult choices and sometimes leads them to forego a key sector such as telecommunications, which is an important medium for the growth of economic activities. The capital cost of telecommunications development as a whole is very high, as regards both purchase and installation of equipment, and maintenance and training in this rapidly developing branch of advanced technology. Some 100 billion dollars are spent in the world each year on extension and modernization of telecommunications. These investments are usually sound since almost all the companies operating telecommunications networks make a profit; the return on fixed assets in service usually exceed about ten percent.[1]

The procedure for capital investment in industrialized countries to develop the telecommunications sector is different from the procedure that is used in African countries. The industrialized countries are the manufacturers of telecommunications equipment, and the companies which operate telecommunications in those countries possess human and financial resources incomparably greater than those of African countries. African countries are compelled to import equipment from industrialized countries and to seek foreign currency to pay for their imports.

The penetration of telephones in Africa is low in comparison to the rest of the world. With 10 percent of the world's population, Africa, excluding South Africa, has no more than approximately 0.4% of the world's telephones. The average telephone density is less than 0.6 lines per one hundred inhabitants compared to 3.5 in Asia and 4.6 in Latin America. The programs of the United Nations Transport and Communications Decade for Africa (1978-1988) set a target penetration of one telephone per one hundred inhabitants by 1988.

Most African countries need to increase the growth rate of their telecommunication infrastructures by about fifty percent to reach an acceptable comparative ratio to the other regions of the world. The Economic Commission for Africa has identified 206 telecommunications projects whose total cost is around $2.7 billion. The search for capital for investment in telecommunications cannot be dissociated from the current difficult economic climate nor from the constraints that this imposes.

There are many sources for the financing of telecommunications development in Africa: suppliers' credits, commercial banks, bilateral governmental aid, and multilateral financing institutions, to name a few of these. The choice of resources should take account of the cost of money, financing conditions and the scale of the projects. Because of a good profit earning capacity, telecommunications projects can use capital lent under normal market conditions. However, this statement must be qualified in view of a number of special problems encountered in African countries, some these problems are:

- shortage of foreign currency
- bad credit rating
- relative neglect of the most isolated areas
- shortage of qualified personnel.

In view of these situations, it would be better for African countries to seek sources of financing which offer softer terms so that the servicing of the debt would be less onerous. Special care should be taken in considering the various sources of capital for telecommunications financing, to ensure that the various economic and financial constraints on the particular country and the operating companies are taken into account.

Investment in PANAFTEL subregional network or even any African country's telecommunications system must be integrated with the overall development strategy, allowing for the interaction between telecommunications and the other branches of the economy. Not all sources of capital are affected by these problems and each subregion or country should mobilize the various resources in accordance with its subregional national development plan.

PANAFTEL has attracted many types of funding from diverse sources. Table 13 provides a synopsis of most often used types of financing and major principal sources, including African Development Bank, European Community, World Bank, Canadian Government, French Government, Japanese Government, British Government, German Government, and United States Government. Funds from suppliers' credits, commercial banks, and private financing institutions have been comparatively easy to mobilize by African governments. They do entail, however, a number of problems; they are often linked to specific kinds of equipment; they involve high interest rates and very short repayment periods; and the cost of equipment acquired with suppliers' credits is always very high. To ensure the return of their funds, these sources sometimes prefer to deal only with specific, highly profitable investments such as international earth stations or international transit centers.

Bilateral government aid takes the form of gifts or loans and usually comes from industrialized countries. These countries have financial institutions which channel their cooperation with African countries. The interest rates tend to be available through political affinities, existing cooperation agreements, or other conditions that link the donor country to the receiving country. The offer of these kinds of resources is often subject to the acquisition of goods and services, at times even specific equipment, from the donor country. This also sometimes means introducing prototypes into the telecommunications network which entail a heavier financial burden and greater technical complications for the administration that has to operate them. Bilateral sources of finance often do not concern themselves with the technical and financial viability of the project under consideration.

The main aim of the multilateral financial institutions is to further the socioeconomic development of the subregion or country. The difficulties encountered by the countries usually arise from the organization and management of the administration in the sectors. Ideally, any real assistance to the countries ought to make the administration vigorous and efficient. That is why in the financing projects, multilateral institutions do not concern themselves merely with the purchase and installation of equipment, they also make an assessment of the executing bodies in order to be able to advise the authorities and help them to obtain the maximum return on their investment.

Table 13

Types and Principal Sources of Financing PANAFTEL Development

Type of Financing	Principal Sources
multilateral financing	African Development Bank (ADB), African Development Fund (ADF), European Community (EEC), Arab Fund, World Bank and International Development Association (IDA), West African Development Bank (WADB), Fund of the Economic Community of West African States (ECOWAS).
bilateral financing	Canada, Denmark, France, Federal Republic of Germany, Iraq, Japan, Kuwait Fund, Netherlands, Norway, Sweden, United Kingdom, United States.
grants	Canada, France, Federal Republic of Germany, Italy, Netherlands, Nigeria, Norway, Sweden, United Kingdom.
financing of studies technical assistance	UNDP, Arab Bank for Economic Development in Africa (DADEA), ITU, Sweden.
internal financing	Most countries utilize, to a greater or lesser extent, internal financing self-generated or derived from government development budgets, as well as suppliers' credits for part of their development program.

Source: *Telecommunications Journal,* 1984, p. 208.

Although most of the PANAFTEL network has attracted financing, especially after the intervention of ECOWAS and the SATCC, there are certain links and implementation stages that still require financing. These are principally in the Central African subregion which requires serious financing. The Central African Post and Telecommunications Conference has taken up this matter and has even set up a special permanent secretariat. Therefore, it is expected that positive action will be taken shortly to finance the remaining links in that subregion.

Countries with sufficient resources have relied often on internal financing for their projects. A few multi-country or single-country projects have been financed by outright grants by donor countries. United Nations Development Program has provided funds for some PANAFTEL systems within its development program and has financed International Telecommunications Union's technical assistance activities in most aspects of the implementation of the PANAFTEL network, including pre-feasibility and pre-investment studies, surveys, and maintenance projects.[2]

CONTRIBUTION OF THE AFRICAN DEVELOPMENT BANK (ADB)

Under its charter, the ADB has two types of resources. The first, called ordinary resources, includes paid-up share capital, funds obtained through loans, funds received as repayment of loans granted, and revenues produced by loan operations. Article 8 of the Agreement establishing the African Development Bank provides that the bank can set up special funds, or agree to manage special funds, intended to serve its objectives within the framework of its functions.

In compliance with these provisions, the African Development Fund (ADF) was created in 1972 and the Nigeria Trust Fund (NTF) in 1976. These two funds are the source of concessional loans, whereas the ordinary resources of the ADB are used for a variety of loans under standard terms and conditions. In order to finance pre-investment studies and detailed technical and design studies, the ADB has established a Technical Assistance Account within the framework of the African Development Fund. These are all the resources of the African Development Bank.

From the time it was established until December 31, 1985, the ADB, which participates directly in the implementation of the Pan-African Telecommunications network, PANAFTEL, has financed twenty-seven telecommunications projects within twenty-one African projects for an overall figure of 251.02 million units of account, equivalent to an equal amount in US dollars. Bearing in mind the generally high profitability of telecommunications projects, loans are normally granted using the ADB's ordinary funds, except in rare cases which take account of some countries' peculiarly difficult situations. Participation of the African Development Bank in telecommunications represents 7 percent of the cumulative commitment of the bank's ordinary resources, which amounted to 3.383 million units of account by the end of 1985, and approximately four percent of the total cumulative commitments of the ADB group.[3]

REGIONAL AFRICA SATELLITE COMMUNICATION SYSTEM (RASCOM)

History was made from February 4 - 6, 1991, at the African Telecommunications Ministers Conference held in Abuja, Nigeria, which approved the RASCOM feasibility report. One of the most important decisions of the ministers, was to proceed immediately to the implementation phase which consists of two stages: namely, the transitional stage and the operational stage. A fifteen-member Committee of Country Experts (CCE) was established to be responsible for the supervision of the transitional stage and thus direct the work of RASCOM Interim Office. The conference agreed to a dedicated satellite system as a viable option for the African countries.

An institutional framework was also adopted by the Conference for the transitional stage. An Inter-Agency Coordinating Committee, composed of the OAU chairman, ECA chairman, African Development Bank, ITU, Pan-African Telecommunications Union, United Nation Development Project, and United Nations Education Scientific Cultural Organization, was responsible for carrying out the feasibility study.

As of November 21, 1991, the total contribution for RASCOM has mounted to US$535,968.94 as forty-one African countries successfully created the RASCOM organization. The countries that participated in the initial investment are shown in Table 14.

Regional African Satellite Communications System and the INTELSAT have committed themselves to work together to enhance communications throughout Africa. The commitment was to endorse a complete plan to consolidate all the African domestic network presently using the INTELSAT system. At the moment, African nations lease capacity from INTELSAT which is spread among six different satellites. The objective of RASCOM is, therefore, to pool all the existing transponder capacity for domestic and regional services onto only two satellites.[4]

Commitment from both sides has been established to improve interconnectivity and the telecommunications infrastructure of Africa as a whole, which will, therefore, integrate and set a standard for communications within the African continent for years to come.

Table 14

COUNTRY CONTRIBUTIONS
FOR RASCOM TRANSITIONAL STAGE

Received Country Contributions (in order of receipt)

No.	DATE	COUNTRY	CONTRIBUTION	
1.	05.03.91	Benin	US $	10,000
2.	19.03.91	Burkina Faso	US $	10,000
3.	25.03.91	Cameroon	US $	50,000
4.	09.04.91	Nigeria	US $	99,970
5.	17.04.91	Ghana	US $	38,352.62
6.	25.04.91	Niger	US $	9,985
7.	30.04.91	Chad	US $	10,152.28
8.	08.05.91	Central African Republic	US $	10,000
9.	17.05.91	Zimbabwe	US $	20,000
10.	27.05.91	Gambia	US $	10,000
11.	07.06.91	Uganda	US $	9,978.95
12.	17.06.91	Madagascar	US $	10,000
13.	11.06.91	Mali	US $	10,000
14.	26.06.91	Cote d'Ivoire	US $	32,625.48
15.	02.07.91	Guinea Bissau	US $	9,982.52
16.	08.07.91	Lesotho	US $	10,000
17.	26.07.91	Kenya	US $	50,000
18.	05.08.91	Malawi	US $	10,000
19.	16.08.91	Zambia	US $	10,000
20.	21.08.91	Sao Tome & Principe	US $	10,000
21	27.08.91	Ethiopia	US $	10,000
22.	27.08.91	Tunisia	US $	10,000
23.	23.09.91	Swaziland	US $	10,000
24.	30.09.91	Congo	US $	10,000
25.	01.10.91	Egypt	US $	9,922.09
26.	01.10.91	Tanzania	US $	10,000
27.	09.10.91	Senegal	US $	15,000
28.	30.10.91	Mauritius	US $	10,000
29.	14.11.91	Burundi	US $	10,000
30.	21.11.91	Guinea	US $	10,000

TOTAL   **US $ 535,968.94**

Note: Date presented as date.month.year.
Source: *RASCOM Bulletin*, December 1991, RASCOM Interim Office, ITU, Geneva.

CHAPTER V

NOTES

1. Bihute, D. "Sources of Investment Capital for Telecommuni-
    cations." Paper presented by the Vice-President of the African
    Development Bank at the African Telecom '86 Conference.
    Nairobi, Kenya: African Development Bank, 1986.

2. Tedros, G. "The development of the Pan-African Tele-
    communication Network (1960-1983)." *Telecommunications
    Journal,* 51 (4), 1984, pp. 204-210.

3. Apetey, K. "New Strategies for Telecommunication Financing in
    Developng Countries." Paper presented at the International
    Forum (Telecommunications for Development) in New York
    City; Sponsored by the INTELSAT (October 1986).

4. International Telecommunications Union. *RASCOM Bulletin.*
    ITU, Geneva (December 1991).

CHAPTER VI

Summary and Analysis

This chapter provides a brief summary and analysis of the development of telecommunications in Africa since the introduction of the Pan-African Telecommunications network. The trend towards international, subregional, and regional integration of communication facilities and services has been examined, as has the trend towards modernization of the African telecommunications systems. The study notes, from the historical analysis of the development of PANAFTEL, growing awareness among African governments of the significance of telecommunications in contemporary society and, therefore, the potentially significant contribution of PANAFTEL to Africa's socioeconomic development. The study concludes by anticipating a total regional approach to PANAFTEL development. Such approach, in the author's opinion, would facilitate rapid economic development of the entire African region. The author further makes recommendations to support the goals of African development.

PANAFTEL TECHNOLOGICAL CAPABILITIES AND OPERATIONS

Telecommunications institutions are beginning to play a fundamental infrastructural role in promoting development activities in every sector of the African economy. PANAFTEL is significantly improving the number of telephones, telex, and other transmission media in service, as well as the number of subscribers to these services. These numbers and how they are related are the usual yardsticks for measuring the available quantity and quality, as well as the extent of use, of telecommunications services. The PANAFTEL network has significantly improved the availability of telecommunications services in Africa by achieving its primary objective of providing national and international computer communication services, telephone services with advanced features, black and white television transmission and reception services, facsimile services, and teleconferencing applications. The implementation of this primary objective of PANAFTEL has been quickening the pace of change in the availability of technology services and has been widening the range of technical service options and choices available to Africans and African countries. The future offers improved service quality and more technological capabilities to most African countries at lower cost.

With respect to the PANAFTEL technologies and operations, this study found that the need for a Pan-African telecommunications network was recognized in Dakar, in 1962 at the first meeting of the Regional Plan Committee of Africa. Since its conception, PANAFTEL development, up to the end of 1990, has encompassed the following:

- 43,000 km of transmission links
- 35,000 microwave facilities
- 8,000 km of submarine cables
- supplementary satellite communication earth stations in 41 countries
- 43 international switching centers, and
- 42 international telex exchanges.

PANAFTEL is divided into four operational subregional groups: North Africa, West Africa, Central Africa, South and East Africa. With very few deficiencies, PANAFTEL is now capable of connecting all the African countries without routing through Europe or North America. These developments resulted from the cooperative efforts of various regional, subregional, and international organizations, together with multilateral and bilateral financial institutions.

In order to make recommendations to foster the evolution of the telecommunications infrastructure in Africa, the development of earth stations for domestic and international use of the INTELSAT system in the African region was reviewed, in addition to regional satellite networks such as those of the Arab Satellite Organization (ARABSAT) which has linked the Northern African countries. PANAFTEL's interconnection to the global network was also reviewed with detailed analysis of operational and financial involvement by African telecommunication administrators and other organizations.

MAJOR CONSTRAINTS

The major factors that impact negatively on the PANAFTEL network are financial, structural, administrative, and political. Although these factors are interrelated, they can be discussed separately.

1. Financial and Economic Constraints

Financing PANAFTEL development calls for considerable outside resources. Whether private, bilateral, or multilateral, it is important for funds to be mobilized from all sources. On behalf of the PANAFTEL coordinating committee and in pursuance of Resolution CM/Res. 885 (XXXVII) of the OAU Council of Ministers, the African Development Bank convened the first meeting of multilateral financial institutions for the PANAFTEL project and the United Nations Transport and Communications Decade in Africa. The meeting held in Abidjan on September 13-15, 1982, reached the following conclusion:

> "The meeting observed that multilateral institutions have more funds available in comparison with the official requests related to tele- communications which have been presented to them. Considering the evident need of resources for development of telecommunications, member states are urged to take the necessary steps for the utilization of the resources. Regional organizations can play a significant role in these matters."[1]

On the basis of past experience, it is apparent that the financing of maintenance and training are critical factors in the effective operation and further development of telecommunications projects. It is an established fact that a well-organized and properly managed sector is a more favorable prospect for potential funding and future financial support.

2. Structural Constraints

The initial concept of the PANAFTEL network as providing international links and switching centers was modified in June 1981 by the OAU Council of Ministers for the purpose of accelerating interconnection of national networks and to launch PANAFTEL as a complete continental telecommunications network. Setbacks to a fully operational PANAFTEL network included:

- inadequate finance for purchase of spare parts
- absence of adequate maintenance
- deficient tariffs and transit agreements
- inadequately equipped international switching terminals
- lack of coordinated signaling systems.

The guiding goal of this study was to develop the rationale for and to generate an advocacy of regional cooperation and development of telecommunications systems in the African region. In developing this rationale, the general concept of the PANAFTEL infrastructure was explained and its role to support African economic development was discussed. An overview of the fundamental problems which have hindered telecommunications development in the African region was presented.

However, the current problems stemming from the social, technical, environmental, and political aspects are central to future development of telecommunications in Africa.

3. Political and Administrative Constraints

There is a direct formal and informal relationship between the PANAFTEL technological infrastructure and public policymaking in Africa, like anywhere else. PANAFTEL, thus, influences all political and economic activities in the African region. The inability of some African telecommunications organizations to manage their services effectively, the failure to control the development of the systems, and the absence of managerial and policymaking skills for the implementation of some of the objectives of PANAFTEL have resulted in ineffective investment, delay in project execution, underutilization of facilities, and excessive operating costs.

The consequence of the above factors is that PANAFTEL has been operating below capacity. In effect, the contributions of telecommunications, as a public utility, to the welfare of each African economy has been reduced in three ways:

1. The revenues generated have been kept within the limits imposed by a particular country's lack of capacity and the inadequacy of telecommunications interconnections.

2. The revenues available from commercial and industrial enterprises have been affected adversely by that country's inability to provide them with the much-needed telecommunications services.

3. The failure of that African country's telecommunications organizations to exploit the full potential of the PANAFTEL ability to assist the government in providing other economic opportunities has placed arbitrary limits on telecommunications applications in that country. These arbitrary limits and failures usually result from the decisions of governments that feel politically insecure.

Presently, telecommunications organizations in Africa are confronted with the task of developing a rational approach to the problems of creating an orderly and well-managed private telecommunications organization. With the increased demand by African economies for telecommunications services to support goods and other service enterprises, all African governments are faced with the task of re-examining existing telecommunications policies and or procedures as to their suitability and adaptability. Any policies and procedures that are no longer applicable must be discarded or modified. New policies and procedures must also be introduced to ensure that the capabilities and potentials of PANAFTEL are exploited optimally and maximally.

CHAPTER VI

NOTES

1.   Bihute, D. "Sources of Investment Capital for Telecommuni-
cations." Paper presented by the Vice-President of the African
Development Bank at the African Telecom '86 Conference.
Nairobi, Kenya: African National Bank, 1986.

CHAPTER VII

Conclusions
and
Recommendations

Telecommunications development in Africa lags behind that in other parts of the developing world. The factors behind the sector's slow growth are related primarily to the lack of awareness of the benefits of adequate telecommunications services by the African policy makers. Improved telecommunications can lead to better development, project management, and better utilization of other economic resources.

There is no doubt that a fully developed Pan-African telecommunications network will change the development face of the African society. The PANAFTEL network, with the basics of its design, will also be used as a channel for education, for disseminating information, encouraging self-reliance, strengthening the social fabric and sense of national identity, and contributing to political stability in the region. Based on the outcome of the analysis of the PANAFTEL technologies, operations and associated factors, I put forth the following recommendations:

Recommendation 1

The Pan-African Telecommunication Academy (PANATA) should be established to plan and support the development of telecommunications among African nations. All member nations should be committed to supporting this timely institution, with the understanding that implementation of its recommendations would require ratification by the governing bodies of each nation.

PANATA should come directly under the International Telecommunications Union, the Organization of African Unity, and the Economic Commission for Africa. As soon as possible, the academy should address the training and retraining of telecommunications technologists in the application of science and economics for the self-reliance of African nations. This academy should train not only high-level executives, consultants, and engineers, but also competent technicians whose experience in modern telecommunications systems would support the PANAFTEL's future institution on advanced technology.

Recommendation 2

Reasonable financial support from the developed INTELSAT member countries to the developing ones will boost African international telecommunications. It is recommended, therefore, that developed INTELSAT member countries establish funds to finance satellite earth stations and terrestrial facilities of the PANAFTEL for the African INTELSAT member countries.

Recommendation 3

Dramatic technological advancement is taking place at a time when the development role of telecommunications is more important than ever. In essence, no development program of any African country will be balanced, integrated, or efficient unless it fully utilizes the available PANAFTEL technical capabilities. African governments should exert less — or no — political influence on their telecommunications organizations to enable them to compete more effectively with other major international telecommunications organizations for profit. It is, therefore, recommended that African governments allow their telecommunications organizations to operate as private multinational corporations so that they can compete on national and international levels by making maximum use of the PANAFTEL network.

The governments of both industrialized nations and those of African countries need to recognize their fundamental interest in implementing and expanding the PANAFTEL network worldwide. The subregional and national networks should be made more efficient and self-reliant. The benefits of the technologies associated with PANAFTEL should be fully exploited. All the recommendations that have been made are based on the analysis of the African telecommunications situation. *There is no single solution; a range of new policies and actions is necessary at the same time.* Time is on PANAFTELs's side, after all — "Rome was not built in a day."

Index